DUE DATE			
JUN = 1 1988			
MAY 3 1 1988			
	201-6503		Printed in USA

The Car Solution

THE CAR SOLUTION

The Steam Engine Comes of Age

GARY LEVINE

HORIZON PRESS  New York

Contents

Illustrations

Introduction

Every person who reads these pages has been endangered in one way or another by the three major crises, all related to the motor vehicle, which have afflicted modern society.

The most widely publicized has been the energy crisis because its effects on our lives—in our hospitals and schools, our homes and factories, stores and food supplies—have been the most immediately dangerous and widespread.

The crisis of air pollution which preceded the energy shortage, still a staggering problem though not so widely recognized, is just as serious and just as urgent. The number of deaths, and of lives continuously shortened by poison in the atmosphere, is immeasurable. The terrible effects on our children are still to be grasped. Some sense of the enormity of the evils may be gained from the official reports documented in later pages of this book.

The third crisis, doubtless the least understood of all though it is just as urgent, has been attacked as "insidious" in a

300-page report for the government which states that it may affect *at least 80 million Americans*. It is noise pollution. The documentation which nails down the dangers of deafness and the description of the indifference of car manufacturers who are consciously offering features which intensify these dangers are also given in later pages.

The sum of these crises is simple and terrifying: Though we may be aware of the sacrifices we are asked to make, and may even be temporarily resigned to making, we are not (certainly not enough of us) equally aware that our lives are being irreparably damaged. But this "insidious" process goes on whether we are aware of it or not. The rampant dangers of the internal combustion engine are universally recognized.

What are we doing? The average citizen, despite the flood of news, may with some measure of justice say he doesn't know enough about it. The conditions are really too complicated. What, then, are the experts, or those we have elected to power, with access to the facts, and with conscience, doing to save lives? How soon will we—if not we, our children—be able to live in some semblance of the sanity that uncontrolled manipulators of technology have eroded? How soon will conditions conducive at least to a restoration of health be possible? The directors of the car-producing corporations are not optimistic. Responsible government officials are pessimistic. It is only at rare moments that we hear ideas expressed with the imagination and flexibility that seem to come alive in the absence of vested interest—ideas that spring from vision and conscience as well as from the recognition of feasibility.

When the disastrous fuel crisis began, one of the wisest observers of human affairs in our time, E. B. White, said in *The New York Times*: "The internal-combustion engine has had its little day; we should return now to the incomparable steam engine, which has only a few moving parts, is quiet, does not pollute, and gives one the sense of flying."

Moved by the earlier crisis of air pollution Steward Udall, former Secretary of the Interior to two Presidents, wrote: ". . . Detroit still must recognize that the time has come to begin developing external combustion engines, like the steam engine. . ."

The major factor in the overwhelming advantages of the steam engine is that it is capable of using fuels which are not only much cheaper but also readily available—among them: kerosene, alcohols, coal gas and even coal itself.

The signs of direction are unmistakable. Objective opinion is being expressed increasingly in the press and on the air on the advantages of the steam engine, about which silence seems to be maintained by those whose interests are involved with the internal combustion engine and its trail of crises.

The Car Solution: The Steam Engine Comes of Age: As the title suggests, I believe that all the evidence points to the steam engine as our hope. But it is also the purpose of this book to tell its complete story; the fascinating persistence in its development for many years despite its failures; the reasons for both its failures and successes so as to enable us to profit by the lessons to be learned from its true history; to show what is being done today in the making of steam engines; and to demonstrate at last the reasons for a hopeful future in solving our travel and transportation needs and maintaining our health as well.

Early Adventures With
Self-propelled Vehicles

First, some official views of the problem:

Dr. A. J. Haagen-Smit, Chairman of the Task Force on Air Pollution has stated: "Restoring and preserving the nation's air quality is a monumental task which requires the active cooperation of all levels of government."[1] Few will deny that the internal combustion engine "is the single largest source of air pollution in the United States."[2] The National Academy of Sciences claims that emissions from gasoline engines cannot be controlled to meet Environmental Protection Act standards."[3]

Former E.P.A. Administrator William D. Ruckelshaus reported that if the situation persists the air quality of many major American cities may not meet 1975 standards.[4] In this context, Stewart Udall's statement, already quoted, bears re-emphasis: "Detroit still must recognize that the time has come to begin developing external combustion engines like the steam engine . . ."[5]

Early Adventures With Self-propelled Vehicles

Prompted by California's steam bus project, the federal government has acted. As early as 1968, the Senate Commerce Committee held hearings to determine the steam car's role in solving the pollution problem and were impressed by their findings.[6] By March, 1970, the Urban Mass Transportation Administration approved a grant for the development of three different types of steam propulsion systems to be used in buses.[7] After more than forty years steam power has been revived and with it a solution to our most serious environmental problem.

I

The steam-powered land vehicle, though it has until recent years failed—for reasons which will become clear—has had an interesting history. Though it is a history in which Americans play a prominent role, the story of steam vehicles begins in seventeenth century Europe when several inventors built steam-powered contraptions. In 1601, the Italian chemist Giovanni Battista della Porte wrote a treatise in which he described a simple steam pump.[8] Some thirteen years later Solomon de Caus, a French engineer, simplified della Porte's pump by building a model in which one vessel served as both boiler and displacement chamber.[9] By 1629, the Italian physicist Giovanni Branca had described a steam turbine in which steam propelled the vanes of a horizontal wheel.[10]

It was not until 1662, however, that Edward Somerset, the second Marquis of Worcester, built the first working steam engine.[11] Although no more than a pump in which steam from one vessel displaced water in another, it could raise four large buckets of water to a height of forty feet in less than four minutes.[12]

It was during this period that the first automobile was built in China, then isolated from a scientifically progressive Europe. In 1655, Father Ferdinand Verbiest, a Belgian priest in the service of the Khan, constructed a model carriage propelled by an ancient Greek invention known as an aeolipile.[13] It operated when steam from the aeolipile moved a wheel-like device equipped with vanes which, through gearing, turned the rear wheels.[14]

Some twenty-five years later Sir Isaac Newton, the genius

who explored philosophy, science and mathematics, sketched a steam-powered vehicle which was designed so that steam escaped from the small aperture of a large boiler at such a high velocity that the ensuing reaction would move the vehicle.[15] Obviously the great weight of such a machine would have made it an impressive failure, if it had been built to full-scale.

To the inquiring mind of seventeenth century man, steam-powered pumps, fountains and model carriages were intriguing discoveries which could replace animal and muscle power. Surely these devices, like any good invention, could be improved, but not before certain basic laws were understood and properly applied. Up to this point the achievements of Branca, de Caus and Somerset did not impress anyone. Their steam contraptions, with the exception of Somerset's pump, were only small models used for demonstration purposes. One condition that had to be met before further progress could be achieved was an understanding of the physical properties of matter. In 1682, Sir Samuel Morland, a Cambridge educated mathematician, prepared tables showing how the boiling temperature of water varied with atmospheric pressure.[16] At approximately the same time, Robert Boyle, the brilliant English chemist, discovered the law of gas expansion now known by his name.[17] This new knowledge enabled inventors to make economically useful machines instead of gadgets.

Before long a Dutch mathematician, Christian Huyghens, developed a cylinder fitted with a piston and valve which operated by the explosion of gunpowder.[18] Denis Papins, a student of Boyle and Huyghens, greatly improved this engine by substituting steam for gunpowder, but though he fitted his machine to a model carriage which ran well on a smooth surface, Papins was forced to discontinue his project because of the bad roads and the problems associated with making large cylinders.[19]

It was not until 1699 that a full scale steam engine was built. Thomas Savery, an English mining engineer, was granted a patent on an engine in which steam from one vessel displaced water in another, creating a vacuum. Such a device, it was hoped, could draw water from the pits and mines, but its drawbacks outweighed its advantages.[20] It could draw water only to a height of 160 feet and this limited its use. Also, because it was single-acting, it required two men to operate and their lives were usually in danger because high pressure steam frequently burst the inferior sheet iron boiler.[21]

In 1712 a major step forward was taken by Thomas Newcomen, an obscure ironmonger from Dartmouth, England. The advantages of his invention over Savery's were immediately apparent to the scientific world for here was a self-acting engine that could be operated with relative safety. In operation steam, fed into a large cylinder, drove out the air, creating a vacuum. Atmospheric pressure then pushed the piston down.[22]

Newcomen engines found immediate application in the British mines and in European cities where they operated without difficulty for many years. One writer has claimed that they were used well into the twentieth century. The two at the Westerfield colliery lasted over a hundred years, while the one at the South Liberty colliery was in continuous service for 140 years.[23]

A new chapter in the history of steam power began in 1763, when James Watt, an instrument maker from Glasgow, added a condenser to the Newcomen engine. This made it economical to use, as it saved as much as "75 per cent in fuel."[24] Later he changed the engine into one developing rotative motion and explored ways for using expansive steam. This eventually led him to build a two-cylinder double-acting engine and a steam pressure indicator.[25]

The development of the Newcomen and Watt engines indicated that a stage had been reached where steam power could be successfully applied to road vehicles. Although the engines of the eighteenth century were looked upon as marvellous applications of scientific knowledge to mechanical invention they were too large for road vehicles. The vehicles built by Father Verbiest and Denis Papins were novelties which never advanced beyond the model stage. But in 1786 Watt was granted a patent on a steam carriage which boasted an iron boiler, a double-acting vertical engine, a condenser and a variable speed transmission.[26] The Watt carriage, however, never left the drawing board because its creator felt that high pressure steam would burst the iron boiler and cause injury to the operator.[27] Watt, who was always prejudiced against high pressure steam, applied for a patent to protect his creation from other inventors.[28]

Not everyone was as pessimistic about the future of steam carriages. Dr. Erasmus Darwin, the grandfather of Charles Darwin, devoted more time to this subject than to his medical practice. In the *Botanic Garden* he wrote:

Soon shall thy arm, unconquered steam afar,
Drag the slow barge, or drive the rapid car;
On, on, wide-waving wings expanded bear
The flying chariot through the air.[29]

While Watt was still experimenting with stationary engines the French government had taken steps to build a self-propelled artillery tractor. In 1769, Nicholas Cugnot, an accomplished military engineer, constructed the first full-scale vehicle to move by steam. Weighing five tons, the huge tractor rested on three wooden wheels shod with iron tires. The furnace and boiler were combined into one unit and situated in front of the driving wheel making steering difficult if not impossible. The engine consisted of two single-acting cylinders approximately thirteen inches in diameter and twelve and a half inches long. The pistons moved alternately, working the front wheel by turning pawls and ratchets which converted reciprocating motion into rotary motion. When steam forced the piston down in one cylinder a rocking beam pulled the piston up in the other cylinder. Each time this happened the wheel turned a quarter revolution. Manually operated valves controlled the flow of steam to each cylinder. Reversing the pawls moved the tractor backward.[30] Of very crude design it was described by a French officer as being

. . . capable of 6 miles per hour. As the capacity of the boiler was out of proportion and neither the boiler nor the pumps were made with sufficient precision, the carriage could not run continuously for more than 12 or 15 minutes. It was then necessary to let the car rest for about the same period so that steam could attain its original power . . . The furnace was badly made allowing steam to escape, and the boiler too, appeared too weak to sustain in every case the effect of steam.[31]

The first trial run was observed by a number of prominent

spectators, including the Duc de Choiseul, Minister of War and Cugnot's sponsor. Speeding along at 2¾ miles per hour, the tractor became unmanageable and struck a stone wall.[32] De Choiseul, undeterred by this setback, appropriated 900 pounds for the construction of another vehicle. A second machine appeared in 1771, and whether it was the first one rebuilt or a new one is not known. An improved steering mechanism made little difference in performance, as this time the tractor over-turned. Cugnot, it has been alleged, was arrested and his machine impounded to "keep it out of mischief."[33] Since the Duc de Choiseul was out of political favor, he was quickly exiled to England. He was unable to return until the Consulate period, but his inventive efforts were recognized by Napoleon who gave the aged engineer a pension of 10,000 francs. The First Consul also encouraged him to continue his experiments, but with wagons instead of military vehicles. Nothing further was accomplished and, with Cugnot's death in 1804, the lead in developing steam vehicles shifted to England.[34]

Before the eighteenth century had ended a model steam car was operating on the roads of Redmuth in Cornwall, England. In 1784 William Murdock, James Watt's foreman, constructed a small vehicle of simple design which attracted much attention.[35] It was designed to carry only a driver who sat on a flat board which was supported on three wheels. The boiler, with its small spirit lamp, and the engine were an integral unit situated at the rear. A strong crank axle, the first of its type, was attached to the rear wheels. It turned by the action of a rocking beam and piston rod.[36] Murdock, satisfied with its performance, was prepared to go into production. James Watt and his business partner Matthew Boulton, however, had other ideas and persuaded the inventor to discontinue his work with cars to perfect their huge pumping engines.[37]

The race to produce a marketable steam carriage occupied inventors for the next two decades. In 1786, William Symington, a twenty-one year old Scottish engineer at the Warlock Mines made a practical model of a steam coach.[38] The young inventor's friends were so impressed by his achievement that they persuaded him to exhibit his creation before the scientific community at

Edinburgh.[39] Its engine was comprised of one double-acting cylinder attached directly to the rear axle. Steam pressure, acting on both ends of the cylinder, pushed the piston rod back and forth. This action, in turn, moved a complicated arrangement of racks, chains and pulleys which propelled the coach. Symington's efforts, however, did not go beyond the planning stage. The poor Scottish roads discouraged him from producing another machine and he turned his attention to steamboats.[40]

Between 1786 and 1840 more than forty steam carriages, tractors and drags were built in the British Isles. The combined total for all other nations was nine; France is credited with two, America with six and Bohemia with one. The English had not only taken a commanding lead in building land vehicles, but also developed the railway locomotive and perfected the stationary pumping engine. These engineering developments came in quick succession and the horse as the supreme master of land transportation was soon dislodged.

Working independently, the Britisher Richard Trevithick and the American Oliver Evans developed the high-pressure steam engine, which had the advantage of reduced size without a corresponding loss in power. The beam and air pump, common to the Watt engine, were dispensed with and steam was applied directly to the piston, thus increasing the engine's speed. Engines of this type usually operated with pressures of less than 200 pounds per square inch, while the low pressure of the Watt or Newcomen engine was approximately 15 pounds per square inch.

Undoubtedly, Richard Trevithick was the most capable of the early inventors. An accomplished engineer who was once associated with William Murdock, his activities in constructing and operating pumping engines in England eventually resulted in a legal battle over the validity of the Watt and Boulton patents.[41] Defeated in this struggle, he turned his talents to solving the problems of land transportation. In 1802 he was granted a patent for a steam vehicle built to carry either freight or passengers. Resembling a locomotive, its wooden frame supported a boiler and a smokestack. Little else is known about the vehicle since the only sketch of it was made by Trevithick's son many years later. At Camborne, on Christmas eve, 1802, the machine was put through a rigorous trial run and performed very well. The *Cornwall Gazette and Falmouth Packet*, referring to it as a carriage, reported that

> . . . . a carriage has been constructed containing a small steam engine, the force of which was found sufficient . . . to impel the carriage, containing several persons, amounting to at least a half a ton, against a hill . . . at four miles per hour. Upon a level road it ran eight or nine miles per hour. [42]

Trevithick's achievement, considered little more than a trick, was hardly noticed by the public or scientific community. Undaunted, he built a second machine in 1804 which demonstrated its durability by making long trips without a breakdown. In appearance the new machine was similar to a stagecoach, with the exception that its two rear wheels were ten feet in diameter. The engine, boiler and furnace were at the rear. In operation high pressure steam was fed into a single, double-acting cylinder, while the crankshaft, geared to each of the rear wheels, operated the sliding valve in the cylinder. [43] Exhibited at London, it proved to be a financial disappointment. Two setbacks were enough for the enterprising inventor and he began designing small railway locomotives, a field which promised more success. [44]

At the time the typical British businessman was still not convinced that the application of mechanical power to road vehicles could be profitable. They were more enthusiastic about the new tram cars which were very popular at the mines. To most engineers this form of transportation seemed a practical alternative to land carriages since they made use of rails. In 1804, Trevithick built a locomotive which was immediately purchased by a Welsh colliery. Four years later he constructed an entire railway in London, running a machine of his own design which he called "Catch-Me-Who-Can." [45] As a result of these developments no steam carriages were built in England during the years 1805-1821. [46]

Julius Griffith, an engineer from Brompton, was the first to renew interest in self-propelled land vehicles. His steam coach, built by Joseph Bramah, the eminent lockmaker, was first designed to carry twelve or more passengers. Hoping to attract investors to their project, the coach was altered to carry three tons of freight. Weighing close to four tons the giant machine was never successful because of a defective boiler which made it difficult to retain water in the lower tubes.[47]

This setback did not discourage others and a short time later two Scotsmen, Thomas Burstall and John Hill, built a huge coach possessing an ingenious method of gearing which permitted "the fore and hind wheels to adapt themselves to the curves of the road."[48] The patent described a flash-type boiler designed to heat trays of water to 500 degrees Fahrenheit.[49] Luke Herbert, a contemporary observer, declared that, "a great deal of time was lost and expense incurred by the repeated failure of the boiler."[50] An explosion at Edinburgh in 1824 forced the two inventors to discontinue their work.

In December, 1824, engineer David Gordon was granted a patent for a carriage which was propelled by iron legs. According to one writer the machine

> ran on three wheels; one in front to steer by and two behind to carry the chief weight. . . . The propelling-rods were formed of iron tubes filled with wood to combine lightness with strength. To the lower ends of those propelling rods were attached the feet. These feet pressed into the ground in regular succession, by a kind of rolling, circular motion, without digging it up.[51]

Gordon soon found this method of propulsion wanting because it required more steam than the boilers could produce. He went to other designs but his success was always limited.

William H. James, with financial help from Sir James Anderson, had better luck. His horse-ribbed boiler, so-called because it resembled a horses's skeleton, had numerous tubes, an inch in diameter, inserted into two horizontal cylinders, one for water and the other for steam. The James coach featured separate axles and four cylinders, two for each wheel. Each of the 4½ foot long boilers supplied its own engine, enabling the wheels to be driven at different speeds. Also, one boiler would suffice should trouble occur.[52] In March, 1829 one of James's coaches, laden with fifteen passengers, made a seven mile run on a rough road, across Epping Forest and back, achieving speeds of from ten to fifteen miles per hour.[53]

The first of the steam coach builders to achieve widespread fame was Goldsworthy Gurney, a lecturer in chemistry at the Surrey Institute.[54] After much experimentation and "repeated trials at great expense," he produced a road machine propelled by iron legs, which was similar in some respects to David Gordon's machine. Weighing four tons, its two single-cylinder horizontal engines propelled it at speeds of ten miles per hour.[55] The unique boiler was composed of small cylindrical tubes which in turn were screwed into horizontal cast-iron headers. They were joined to two vertical steam separators, also made of cast iron. The tubes were not likely to explode because they were butted together; when the pressure rose above 800 pounds a seam would merely open, not burst. This was not the case with the steam separators, which were hollow and did not possess tubular safety. In June, 1831, while the coach was on exhibit in Glasgow, these separators exploded, seriously injuring two young boys.[56]

Despite their drawbacks Gurney's coaches turned steam on common roads from a dream into a reality. In 1825 an improved model, lacking the iron legs, made the trip from London to Melksham and back, a distance of 85 miles, in ten hours, including all stops.[57] It was a new day for land transportation. But not everyone reacted favorably toward the chemist's invention. Anti-machinery rioters in Melksham damaged the coach and forced the young inventor to take refuge in Bath.[58] Incidents such as this, however, were rare and certainly did not deter Gurney from continuing his work.

The steam coach soon became a familiar sight on English roads and others were quick to follow Gurney into what appeared to be a profitable venture. Quick to earn prominence in steamcoaching was Walter Hancock, an able engineer who had nine coaches operating during the years 1824-1836.[59] These machines possessed features which were considered quite advanced for their day. The "sheet-flue" boiler was really a series of flat chambers, arrayed side by side, and heated by flames from a fire-grate. This arrangement was attached by short, verti-

cal tubes to a larger horizontal pipe situated on top of the boiler.[60]
John Farey, the most respected authority on steam in Great
Britain, claimed that Hancock's boilers were lighter and more
practical than any type then in use.[61] Steamcoach enthusiast
Francis Maceroni commented that Hancock's creations were

> certainly and evidently safer than Gurney's coaches. The great
> external horizontal chambers and vertical separators of the latter,
> contain all the water of the boiler, except the comparatively small
> portion held by the one inch tubes which are exceedingly the
> stronger; so that the bursting of a separator or horizontal chamber
> becomes a serious affair.[62]

An upright two-cylinder engine was attached to the crankshaft
and transmitted power to the rear axle through a huge chain.
Vehicle speed in a sharp turn was controlled by a clutch which
was attached to an exterior part of one wheel.[63]

Each coach was a masterpiece of design. In the case of
the Infant, built in 1831, the boiler, furnace, engines and passengers were suspended on heavy leaf springs. A strong crankshaft
and an axle cleverly designed to hold weight gave the vehicle
many trouble-free miles.[64] Its engines, in complete view of the
engineer, were totally encased to protect them from dust and
dirt. Other coaches were also built on this design. The Autopsy,
built in 1833, proved quite popular on the London to Islington
run. It could easily haul three omnibuses and a stage coach,
with fifty passengers, at speeds of from ten to fourteen miles
per hour.[65] Hancock's coaches were capable of carrying from
ten to twenty-two passengers; all had a three man crew which
included a driver, a stoker and a mechanic.[66] By 1836 these
huge machines were running to Stratford, Islington and Padding-
ton and during a five month period made 700 trips, carrying
12,000 passengers over 4,200 miles.[67]

The activities of Gurney and Hancock did not go without
notice. A contest now ensued between the coach builders which
made steamcoaching a popular enterprise. Among the enthusiasts
was the wealthy merchant Sir Charles Dance who in 1837 drove
from London to Brighton towing a fifteen seat omnibus in 5½
hours. He made the return trip in less than five hours.[68] Two

years earlier his carriage ran for a five month period between Cheltenham and Gloucester, carrying 3,000 passengers over 3,500 miles. The nine mile distance was usually traveled in 55 minutes.[69] Although new to the field, merchants Nathaniel Ogle and William Summers boasted of reaching speeds of 35 miles per hour and on one occasion their coach carried nineteen passengers up a steep grade at fifteen miles per hour.[70] Colonel Francis Maceroni, former aide-de-camp to the King of Naples, with financial help from John Squire, built a safe, water-tube boiler consisting of 81 upright tubes. Working pressure was 150 pounds per square inch, but it was claimed the pressure could be raised to 1,050 pounds without an explosion. Equipped with two cylinders geared directly to the rear axle, the vehicle went 1,700 miles without any major repairs.[71] According to Alexander Gordon the Maceroni coach was "a fine specimen of indomitable perseverance."[72]

The advantages of the new mode of transportation were obvious to everyone. People could travel farther, faster and more freely than ever before. The journey from London to Brighton, a distance of 52 miles, took two days by horse-drawn coach. This included a stop-over at an inn where the passengers rested for the night. The steam coach reduced travel time for this rigorous trip to five hours.[73] Of course the steam coach proprietor also made money on his enterprise. Although it cost him 800 £ to build his machine (600 £ more than a horse-drawn coach), operating costs per mile were only 4d—four shillings and three pence cheaper than the horse-drawn competition.[74] His fares were half that charged by the horse coach proprietor and this made him a threat to the established horse interests.[75] In 1831, a select committee of the House of Commons reported that

> . . . the substitution of inanimate for animal power, in draught on common roads, is one of the most important improvements in the means of internal communication ever introduced.[76]

Not everyone agreed with the House report; opposition came from several quarters. Horse coach proprietors were the first to suffer and became the major opponents to steam on Britain's roads. Farmers feared the huge machines would ruin the roads and harm the lucrative traffic in horses. They also believed this would eventually effect the oats market and cause an economic calamity. Coachmen and postboys saw a decrease in the number of available jobs while country gentlemen believed the steam coach was a menace to person and property.[77] The evidence provided to the Select Committee of the House proved these apprehensions unfounded. Alexander Gordon, David's son, who was a prominent engineer and authority on steam coaches, declared that

> . . . the cheap and expeditious mode of conveying passengers and carrying everything to market would eminently tend to the welfare of all classes . . . that coach proprietors would get more custom by carrying people at half the present prices, and would require less capital than in the present uncertain outlay for horses; and that coachmen and boys and horsekeepers would also be benefitted as more men are employed about a steam than horse coach.[78]

Appeals to reason had little effect on the members of Parliament. By 1830, a number of bills were already enacted which levied tolls on steam carriages of from six to twelve times more than their horse drawn counterparts.[79] Not satisfied with their success, the opposition dumped large stones on the roads, seriously damaging at least one of the huge vehicles.[80] While the struggle ensued between the two forces, the Select Committee of the House, after hearing much testimony from both sides, reported that

> 1. . . . carriages can be propelled by steam on common roads at an average rate of 10 miles per hour.
> 2. That at this rate they conveyed up to 14 passengers.
> 3. That their weight . . . may be under three tons.
> 4. That they can ascend and descend hills of considerable inclination with facility and safety.
> 5. That they are perfectly safe for passengers.
> 6. That they are not nuisances to the public.
> 7. That they will become a speedier and cheaper mode of conveyance than carriages drawn by horses.
> 8. That . . . the roads are not acted upon so injuriously as by the feet of horses.
> 9. That rates of toll have been imposed on steam carriages which

would prohibit their being used on several lines of road, were such charges permitted to remain unaltered.[81]

These findings did not alter the situation. The tolls remained and no effort was made to pave the roads. Several steam coach companies had already failed by 1832 and investors were reluctant to contribute any further capital to an enterprise that was harshly penalized by Parliament. In 1831 Goldsworthy Gurney petitioned the House of Commons for 16,000 pounds to enable him to continue his research. Although the Select Committee acceded to the coachmaker's request the Treasury refused to pay the sum.[82] The latter's decision was greatly influenced by the horse lobby and allegations that Gurney was an incompetent engineer.[83]

Another and more serious danger to the steam coach came from the railroad, which could avoid the poor roads and prohibitory tolls. The public, preferring a safe and smooth ride, made the locomotive the most popular form of land transportation. The era of the steam coach was over by 1840, although a few continued to experiment with self-propelled vehicles. In 1834, John Scott Russell, a Scottish engineer, ran coaches between London and Kew and between Glasgow and Paisley.[84] A powerful two-cylinder engine and a large fire-tube boiler gave the coaches sufficient power to haul their own coal tenders, an omnibus and carry 26 passengers.[85] Russell's coach service proved popular for a number of years until prohibitory tolls and opposition from the turnpike proprietors forced him to discontinue service.[86] In 1841, the General Steam Carriage Company ran a coach between a London hotel and Regent's Park, but stayed in business only a year.[87]

Seventeen years passed before another steam carriage was built. Thomas Ricketts, an ironmonger from Stratford, joined with J.E. McConnell of the London and Northwestern Railway to build a small three seat vehicle for the Marquis of Stafford.[88] The three-wheeler had a locomotive type boiler and a horizontal two-cylinder engine which propelled it at ten miles per hour. A second vehicle was built in 1859 and purchased by the Duke of Sutherland.[89] Both men, it appeared, saw the steam carriage as a plaything and this view of self-propelled machines was to remain unchanged for many years.

In spite of the restrictions placed on steam coach builders, progress in design and engineering was discernible over the years. This all ended with the Locomotive Act of 1865. Considered to be the most restrictive piece of legislation concerning self-propelled vehicles ever passed, it required a man with a red flag to walk twenty yards in front of a vehicle whose speed was limited to four miles per hour.[90] The "Red Flag Law" stopped further development of the automobile in England for thirty years.

The advances in technology previously discussed laid the foundation for the modern automobile. By 1830, the water-tube and fire-tube boilers, although capable of much improvement, were proven safe and practical.[91] Steam engines came in a variety of shapes and sizes, the most popular types being oscillating cylinder or two-cylinder double-acting. The conversion of reciprocating motion was achieved by the clever application of cranks, while ratchets, pawls, racks, pinions, chains or belts were used to transfer power. It must be remembered, however, that the science of metallurgy was in its infancy and welding was still a primitive art. As a result inventors were constantly strengthening axles, gears, tubes and frames by increasing their size. Thus an unending cycle was created which only led to bigger coaches, some weighing as much as four tons. Of course paved roads would have altered this situation considerably. Every coach builder knew that the power needed to pull a load on a smooth surface was half as much as that required on a rough one. Climbing a steep hill required twelve times more power and proved to be a severe strain on the boiler and engine.

It was under these circumstances that the steam automobile evolved. The course of events indicated that it should have been further developed in Great Britain or France. The former led the world in manufacturing and technological progress while the latter was the recognized leader in technical education. Strangely enough the steamer was to come into its own in the United States, a nation with a vast land area, few roads and limited technical knowhow.

Backyard Tinkers

Stationary engines, locomotives and steamboats played an important part in settling the American nation. Steam carriages, on the other hand, had a small and insignificant role. Competition from the railroads and a reluctance among businessmen to support machines capable of breaking down, catching fire or exploding inhibited their development, especially during the nineteenth century.

Contrary to popular belief interest in the application of steam was not widespread in British America.[1] In fact Americans saw the steam engine as a large, complex apparatus likely to explode and this view never changed throughout the steam age. The first steam engine in the colonies, erected in 1753 at the Schuyler Copper mine near Passaic, New Jersey, burned twice and was considered no more than a "tourist attraction."[2] During the late 1750's three Newcomen engines, smuggled from England, were operating in the colonies.[3] In 1773 Christopher Colles, a hydraulic engineer employed by a Philadelphia distillery, built the first steam engine in America.[4] Within two years he had designed an improved machine for pumping water to New York City, but the loss of Manhattan Island to the British prevented it from being used.[5] Throughout the postwar years and early national period a small group of Americans continued to produce machines operated by steam. In 1785, John Fitch, an eccentric Connecticut mechanic, operated a model steamboat on the Schuylkill River, which was a topic of interest even in Europe.[6] Of course the first practical steamboat was built by Robert Fulton some twenty-two years later. It is not surprising, therefore, that a working steam carriage was developed in America before 1800.

During the early years of the republic three inventors experimented with steam-powered vehicles. As early as 1786, Oliver Evans, a Philadelphia millwright, applied to the Pennsylvania legislature for a "protective license" to operate a steam carriage but was turned down by a special committee which considered him to be insane.[7] The Maryland legislature, however, was more sympathetic and, in May, 1787, granted him exclusive rights to develop a self-propelled vehicle.[8] In any event Evans did not build a machine until 1805; the reasons for his delay will be discussed later.

Evans was followed by Nathan Read of Salem, Massachusetts, a Harvard graduate who gave up a medical career to manufacture chains.[9] In 1788, he built a strong, lightweight tubular boiler which was quite advanced for the times. Originally designed for use in ships, it could also be adapted to a small carriage. Within two years he had proved his boiler workable on a small model and was granted a patent on the creation. Although the inventor's sketch leaves much to the imagination one can see that steam was passed through two hollow tubes, each leading to two double-acting cylinders which drove the rear wheels. A steering wheel, the first to be used on a self-propelled vehicle, was attached to the front axle. Driving it though, must have been a nightmare, as it was

> . . . turned with great facility by means of cocks and director. To turn the carriage to (the) right the right-hand cock should be closed, more or less according to the shortness of the right cylinder and consequently retard the motion of the right wheel

27

and at the same time accelerate the motion of the left wheel. To turn the carriage to the left a contrary motion is required.[10]

The third automobile pioneer was Dr. Apollos Kinsley of Hartford, Connecticut, who in 1797 drove America's first full-scale steam carriage on Hartford's streets.[11] Little is known of Kinsley's work with self-propelled vehicles because he conducted his experiments in secret to avoid ridicule. Unfortunately, the work of Evans, Read and Kinsley went unnoticed and had little if any bearing on future steam vehicles. In the eyes of the business and scientific community self-propelled machines were no more than mechanical tricks.

Prior to the Jacksonian period the more successful inventions included the seeding and nail-cutting machines, the power loom, the iron plow and the cotton gin—creations which revolutionized agriculture, the building trades and the textile industry.[12] Conditions were not yet favorable for the widespread use of steam power, however, for America was still a nation of craftsmen and artisans, and the fundamentals of the steam engine were known only to a few. In 1803 only eight engines, all of the Newcomen type, were in operation and they were located in New York City, Pittsburgh, Philadelphia and Boston.[13] The Watt engine was not introduced into America until 1807, when Fulton installed one in his boat.[14]

The most capable American mechanic of the time was Oliver Evans, the Philadelphia millwright mentioned above. Born and educated in Delaware, he was already an accomplished engineer at twenty-two, holding patents on a water pump and flour-milling machinery. After his early setbacks with steam carriages, he devoted himself to developing stationary engines and, in 1794, achieved success with one of high pressure design. In an effort to gain recognition abroad he submitted the plans to English steam engineers who later rejected them.[15] Though the possibility has been suggested there is no evidence to indicate that Richard Trevithick stole them, for his methods of developing high pressure engines were quite different than those of Evans. Some seven years later, while employed by the city of Philadelphia to build dredging machinery, he decided once again to build a self-propelled vehicle. Called the Orukter Amphibolis (amphibious digger) it

> consisted of a heavy flat bottomed boat, 30 feet long and twelve feet abroad, with a chain of buckets to bring up the mud, and hooks to clear away sticks, stones and other obstacles. These buckets were wrought by a small steam engine set in the boat, the small cylinder of which is 5 inches diameter and the length of stroke 19 inches . . . when she was launched we fixed a simple wheel at her stern to propel her through the water.[16]

Its "grasshopper" type engine was a considerable improvement over Watt's beam engine because the piston rod was connected directly to the half beam. The piston thrust was thus transmitted directly to the crankshaft. A small tubular boiler, encased by bricks, supplied enough steam to maintain the high pressure required by this engine. Built at his machine shop, a mile from the Schuylkill River, the vehicle had to be placed on wheels so it could be moved. The front axle turned on a pin and the steering "was probably made possible by means of a long pole, of the type used on wagons."[17] The first attempt to move the behemoth resulted in a broken axle. A replacement was quickly made and on July 14, 1805, the first steam-propelled amphibious vehicle in the world rolled up Market Street to the Center Square Water Works on its way to the river. There was much excitement and Evans's workers charged twenty-five cents to any citizen who came close enough to examine the machine.[18] For two days the thirty foot long man-made monster circled the water works at four miles per hour, causing a mixed reaction from the curious if not frightened spectators. On the river, its performance was less than spectacular. It drew nineteen inches of water and could barely move.[19] Evans's experiments led him to conclude that an

> engine 4 times as powerful could propel a boat 16 feet wide, 90 feet long, drawing 2 feet of water, the weight of which would be 86 tons, equal to 903 barrels of flour, about seven or eight miles per hour through the water, everything being properly and well-constructed.[20]

His conclusions were no doubt correct inasmuch as he was the only man in the country who had a thorough knowledge of the immense possibilities of steam power. To the eyes of the Philadelphia Board of Health, however, Evans's scheme was wasteful and unrealistic, and the young inventor sought help elsewhere.

He approached the officers of the Lancaster Turnpike Company with a plan to build self-propelled machines capable of carrying produce and merchandise from Philadelphia to Columbia, Pennsylvania and back more economically than could be done with horses.[21] For $2,500, he told them, he would construct a wagon capable of carrying one hundred barrels of flour at three miles per hour on level roads and one mile per hour in hilly country. The vehicle would make forty miles a day, completing the trip in two days.[22] The same journey made by horse-drawn wagons took three days.[23]

In an effort to draw investors he distributed a prospectus throughout Philadelphia describing his newly created Experiment Company. His venture would never get further than its inception. A committee of the Lancaster Company, after careful consideration of the plan, concluded that steam wagons were impractical when compared to horses since they were unperfected and would require constant repairs. Costs therefore would be much greater than indicated. Evans claimed that two dollars a day was all that was necessary to keep the steamer running, but that was a small sum when one looked at the poor roads. A vehicle shod with iron tires and suspended on crude springs would have absorbed more than its share of road shocks which would consequently result in many breakdowns.

After Evans's work there was little enthusiasm for self-propelled vehicles. Only with the Jacksonian period, opening about 1830, did an interest arise in technical matters. Several scientific institutions were founded and many were attracted to civil engineering. Coinciding with this technological awakening was a return to steam.[24]

The inventive spirit was reflected in the large number of tinkers who were attracted to self-propelled vehicles. In 1828, the Johnson brothers, proprietors of a small Philadlelphia machine shop, built and operated a small steam wagon which had two driving wheels, eight feet in diameter, and two smaller wheels in front, used for steering. An upright boiler, situated at the rear, provided steam for the single cylinder engine.[25] In the same year William T. James, a New York City machinist, built a small three-wheeler driven by upright cylinders and pistons. An improved model, which appeared a year later, featured rotary cylinders, so designed that one exhausted steam into the other.[26]

Much of the activity with steamers took place in New England. In 1830, Harrison Dyer of Boston constructed a steam carriage equipped with a copper boiler and a circulating pump which kept the water moving at a constant rate.[27] Little else is known of Dyer's vehicle except that it was full-scale. At Lynn, Massachusetts, a year later, Joseph Dixon produced a carriage with two engines working on cranks at right angles to each other. The engine and components, however, proved too advanced for the metallurgy of the time, and Dixon abandoned his project.[28]

Among the more successful inventors was Rufus Porter of Hartford, Connecticut, a former editor of the *Scientific Mechanic*. His carriage was designed with an upright watertube boiler and adjacent steam chests at top and bottom. Miter gearing, similar to that used on the Burstall and Hill carriage, turned the axles, enabling one wheel to go faster than the other.[29] Steam engineers testified to the vehicle's ability to run several times in an open field without breaking down. Unfortunately promotors could not be found, and Porter's attraction to the steam car came to an abrupt end.[30] Credit must go, however, to these tinkers, who despite failure, kept automobile technology alive. Their successors would be able to build upon their discoveries until the steamer was made efficient and reliable.

The first tinker to promote the steam automobile actively on a national scale was John K. Fisher of New York City. Endowed with exceptional mechanical ability and keen business acumen, he achieved wide recognition for his work with self-propelled vehicles.[31] His first machine, built in 1842, showed much promise but was abandoned because of the poor roads.[32] The plank road movement, however, had spread across the nation and by 1851 Fisher was ready to try again.

This time he was able to persuade three prominent journalists to support his venture, which resulted in the formation of the American Steam Carriage Company of New York City, with Fisher acting as secretary. Among the other officers were Henry V. Poor of the *Railroad Journal*, Julius W. Adams of *Appleton's Mechanic's Magazine* and Samuel Fleet of the *American Artisan*. Starting with $100,000 capital and offering 1,000 shares at $100 each, the officers stated that:

> Now a new era is fairly begun. Many thousands of miles of plank roads are already built; and this we regard as the most important new element in the system of locomotion, for cities and short routes, where private carriages and omnibuses, that stop frequently, that cannot be confined upon iron rails, and also for the new and thinly peopled routes upon which the business is not sufficient to pay the interest of railroads . . . The manufacture of locomotives has developed talent and skill; superior tools have been invented . . . and steam engines can now be made much better and cheaper than they could be made sixteen years ago, when the patents of those English inventors expired.[33]

To overcome skepticism Fisher built a four wheel locomotive type steam wagon, capable of fifteen miles per hour on plank roads.[34] Businessmen and the public, however, were still reluctant to invest in the new company. Their hesitation is not difficult to explain since the nation's economy was undergoing a marked change. Past panics and the shortage of English money prompted many to be cautious.[35] Besides, the steamboat and locomotive had taken care of the needs of inland transportation for more than two decades and were proven practical. It was the railroads, however, which dominated American transportation by 1850. With nearly 9,000 miles of track, most of it in New England, rail service was adequate for most of the eastern United States and was expanding at a rapid pace in all directions.[36] The unperfected steam wagon, weighing between four and five tons, therefore, was a big gamble.

The American road system was incapable of handling the weight of a steam-powered vehicle. A typical plank road would have been reduced to splinters under the weight of a five ton steam wagon.[37] Other roads were of such poor quality, consisting of loose gravel and a drainage ditch, that the speed of such giant machines would have been reduced to a snail's pace.[38]

In spite of numerous hardships tinkers continued to build vehicles of every shape and description. Fisher decided to sell self-propelled fire engines, a more rewarding venture. Two were built in 1858, in cooperation with the Novelty Iron Works of New York City and sold to the cities of Philadelphia and New York. Both machines maneuvered well and were capable of running up the steepest inclines.[39]

In 1853, Richard Dudgeon, an accomplished machinist who had already invented a portable hydraulic jack, a squirting oil can and a steamhammer, decided to build a steam wagon. He was not, however, moved by the profit motive in this venture. Being an animal lover he wished to substitute his machine for the mistreated horse.[40] His first vehicle, weighing a ton and a half, with driving wheels 42 inches in diameter, closely resembled a locomotive. Two cylinders, located on the outside, drove the rear wheels.[41] It was made so well that on its first trial run in 1857, it successfully pulled a small barouche at ten miles per hour on a gravel road.[42] One barrel of coal was sufficient to maintain steam for four hours, thus making it more economical than horse-drawn vehicles.

That same year it put in an appearance in New York City, frightening onlookers and panicking the horse population. To prevent a riot the police advised the inventor to return to his home in Locust Valley, Long Island.[43] A short time later the wagon was consumed in the great fire at New York City's Crystal Palace while on exhibit in the annual fair of the American Institute.[44]

In 1866 Dudgeon built a second wagon exactly like the first except for a larger boiler. It also performed well, carrying ten passengers at fourteen miles per hour on "a good wagon road." On a paved road it could travel twenty miles per hour.[45] Despite its promise no buyers could be found. Public acceptance of such vehicles was still far off and Dudgeon had to be satisfied with exhibiting his invention at local fairs and carnivals.

Ever so slowly Americans began to see the advantages of steam-powered vehicles. As early as 1841, five Louisiana planters offered $5,000 to anyone who could invent a steam plow capable of turning ten acres a day.[46] Seventeen years later the New York Agricultural Society offered $250 to any inventor who could build an engine that "would relieve horses in plowing, reaping and tilling the soil."[47] Throughout the country blacksmiths and mechanics busied themselves, but only one workable machine was produced. It showed much promise but the inventor could not find the capital to improve his design and, as a result, no further attempts were undertaken prior to the Civil War.[48]

Steam applied to freight-hauling was another matter altogether. In 1859, Major Joseph Renshaw Brown, a government Indian agent stationed in Minnesota, sought a practical means of getting consignments of food and goods to the Sioux Indians living in the hinterlands.[49] The only means of transportation then available were dog-sleds and when these were unavailable the Indians carried the loads on their backs. Brown gave much thought to the problem and while in New York City engaged Joseph A. Reed of the Novelty Works to build a steam wagon.

The finished product was shipped disassembled to Henderson, Minnesota, where it arrived in the summer of 1860. After a careful reconstruction it was put to use in hauling freight from the steamboat landing to the main street, a mile away.[50] No other purpose could be found for the machine since it was too large and too heavy to negotiate the wild Minnesota country where a few trails and paths served as the state's main arteries of communication. A combination of heavy rain and soft soil could disable the vehicle altogether. In appearance it was

> . . . shaped very much like an old fashioned railroad locomotive. It had but three wheels, however, one on the front for the guiding and two on the sides for driving . . . the drive wheels being some twelve feet in diameter. It is steered by an apparatus in front, similar to the pilot's wheel of a steamboat (only smaller) which is so geared that by turning it with the hand the wheel below is guided with perfect ease. The wagon was so geared that its capacity for speed was limited to two and a half miles per hour.[51]

An improved wagon was ordered which arrived at Nebraska City, Nebraska in July 1862. Designed to operate on the hard level plains along the Platte River, it proved so satisfactory during tests that the citizens of Otoe County appropriated $12,000 for road improvement and bridge construction.[52] Designed with four wheels and a water tank capable of holding fifteen barrels, it could run four hours without a refill. The water, however, added an extra 4,500 pounds to the wagon. In August, Brown's steamer was attached to six wagons with loads weighing a ton and a half each, and proceeded toward Denver. Twelve miles from Nebraska City a crank on the driving shaft broke and the first effort to haul freight by steam wagon ended abruptly.[53]

The Civil War and the coming of the railroad put an end to steam wagons in the west. During this period Brown lost most of his property in the Sioux Indian War of 1862, and it was not until 1869 that he could again devote his attention to transportation. Hewrote, "I am now constructing the third steam wagon I have built in this city. . . . Now the completion of the St. Paul and Pacific Railroad to the Red River Valley . . . opens a field for steam wagon operations that cannot be surpassed in any portion of the northwest."[54] The new Wagon was designed to carry five tons of freight at five miles per hour with its four small engines, but Brown died before it was completed.[55]

Others were equally enthusiastic about the use of steam wagons for transport. In 1864 Jesse Frye asked Congress for a grant of land and funds to finance a steam transit line on which steam wagons would replace animal trains on the Santa Fe trail from Independence, Missouri to New Mexico.[56] Frye believed that his steamers could make the rigorous two to three month trip in six days.

A wagon was built in 1864 at the Novelty Works and demonstrated in Brooklyn before a large crowd of observers. In attendance was Major-General William F. Smith of the Army Engineers who predicted that the inventor would "have no trouble getting aid from Congress and the capitalists."[57] Smith was wrong and Frye, without financial help, was forced to drop his project.

In 1868 Oliver Burdette and Robert Webb suffered the same fate and were unable to sell three steam wagons they had built near New Athens, Ohio.[58] The efforts of those who promoted the British-made Thompson steam road locomotive also ended in failure. Built under license in the United States by the Great Locomotive Works of Paterson, New Jersey, it featured an upright boiler with a long smokestack and rubber-shod iron wheels. The new tires probably made a difference in both ride and speed and it was reported that the wagon could travel ten miles per hour pulling twenty tons of freight.[59] Dirt in the moving parts, however, caused frequent breakdowns and this did little to promote sales.

It seemed that tinkers were unable to find a way to correct the mechanical problems which were so common to these machines and this made them unpopular with farmers. Those who could afford these contraptions found them to be a mechanic's nightmare and soon returned to the horse. As a result they did not become important to American agriculture until the 1880's. Nevertheless they played a vital role in the development of the steam automobile and attracted wide interest from many quarters. Henry Ford, at twelve, was so fascinated by one of these machines that forty-seven years later he could recall the name of the driver and the precise number of engine revolutions per minute.[60]

The self-propelled fire engine was to have a more successful and rapid growth than the steam wagon. Following the example set by John Fisher, the Latta brothers furnished the city of Cincinnati with several new engines, thus making it the first municipality in the country to rely on this type of apparatus.[61] Most city councilmen, though, still greeted these machines with skepticism and it took considerable time before they were accepted.

After the Civil War most large cities still relied on horse drawn steam or hand pumpers which threw a stream of water approximately 100 feet. In any event fire engines, whether horse drawn or self-propelled, were expensive and complicated and voices favoring them were usually drowned out.

Leading the country in the production of pumpers of all types was the Amoskeag Manufacturing Company of Manchester, New Hampshire, which had built more than 550 machines between 1859 and 1876.[62] The Amoskeag machine shops were widely known for their products and engineering versatility. They had already built a reputation making locomotives, power looms and textiles; fire engines were an unprofitable sideline. For more than ten years Nehemiah Bean, Amoskeag's chief engineer, had worked on a self-propelled pumper, and the opportunity to show off his invention came with the great Boston fire of November 9, 1872.

Accounts indicate that an epidemic of "influenza epizootic" among the fire horses had incapacitated much of the city's fire department.[63] Downtown Boston was burning and hearing of the disaster Bean drove his gleaming brass pumper from Manchester to help prevent the fire from spreading.[64] Right before the eyes of the Bostonians was the most formidable fire engine ever to appear on an American street. Supported on four six foot high wooden wheels and weighing more than 16,000 pounds, it was powered by two two-cylinder reversible engines which generated more than thirty horsepower. A five foot four inch high boiler had 311 tubes that produced a steam pressure of nearly 200 pounds per square inch.[65] Its quadruple pumps threw a stream of water "380 feet through a 2⅜ inch nozzle."[66] Operating the pumper was far easier than had been believed. Describing a later model, Captain J. Cordier stated:

> The chief engineer rides on the fire box of the engine and has directly under his hand the various levers and wheels which start, stop and regulate the speed of the machine. The assistant engineer rides on the driver's seat and by means of the larger steering wheel he steers the machine. . . . The engine can be turned around in an ordinary street with ease. The road driving power is applied from one end of the main crankshaft to an equalizing compound, and two endless chains running over sprocket wheels permit these rear wheels to be driven at varying speeds when turning corners.[67]

The events of November 9 and 10, 1872, in Boston firmly established the reputation of the self-propelled fire engine. Orders for the vehicle poured in from all over the country and from such remote cities as Amour, Russia; Sydney, Australia; and Yokohama, Japan.[68] By 1880 they were in widespread use in spite of their cost and size, the noise they produced which frightened horses and their inability to gain traction on icy roads. The latter problem, however, was partially overcome by the application of steel lugs on the rear wheels.

The half century after the Civil War witnessed an unusually large number of inventions applicable to transportation. Steam engines were made to work more efficiently; valves were strengthened; boilers made safer. It was no longer uncommon to see a mechanic driving a self-propelled platform wagon or buckboard around his workshop to the sound of shouting children or barking dogs. Sylvester H. Roper of Lowell, Massachusetts was among the first to build a light, speedy carriage capable of going twenty miles per hour.[69] Formerly associated with the Amoskeag Company and a protégé of Nehemiah Bean, he had earned a reputation as a master mechanic. Proof of his ability was clear to New Englanders when he drove a small carriage through Boston's streets in 1863.[70] The vehicle was described by the *Scientific American* as an

> ordinary four-wheeled carriage (which) has a boiler sixteen inches in diameter in the rear with a lever regulating the steam and speed extending over the seat in the front. Beneath the boiler is a furnace and in the rear of the boiler is a small water tank. . . . The whole machine is of two horsepower. Two persons take their seat in the carriage and off it starts, the driver guiding the front wheels by means of a crank and with the other hand he can regulate the speed of the engine or stop the carriage in less time than a pair of horses can be brought to a halt.[71]

The carriage generated much interest since it could outperform the horse, weighed only 700 pounds and cost one cent a mile to operate.[72] In the three decades after the Civil War Roper built a number of carriages and at least one velocipede. The latter, a brilliant piece of engineering, is housed in the Smithsonian Institute, Washington, D.C.[73]

The changed attitudes toward the machine heralded a new age in transportation. In 1873 the Reverend J. S. Carhart, an itinerant Methodist preacher from Racine, Wisconsin persuaded George Slauson, a wealthy lumberman, to finance his project to build a steam buggy.[74] His efforts resulted in a small vehicle which the Racine *Journal* described as:

> An ordinary buggy, except the hind part, which is so constructed that the boiler drops through the rear axle tree. The boiler and

engines rest on springs in the rear of the seat. The buggy is steered by means of a lever that turns forward while the tee-rail is used as a brake. . . . To the boiler, which is upright, is attached two one horsepower engines, each engine drives one of the hind wheels. Each wheel and engine is independent of the other.[75]

Weighing only 600 pounds and capable of doing four miles per hour, the vehicle was so simple to operate, Carhart claimed, that it would be particularly attractive to the ladies. When in September of the same year it was driven through the streets of Racine a toot of the whistle was sufficient to scatter horses and citizens.[76] Carhart's trip made front-page news throughout the state and was a topic of discussion among the members of the Agricultural Committee of the state legislature. As soon as it was recognized that a machine of this type could be useful to the agricultural community a bill was introduced which was designed to encourage "the development of transporation patterned after Reverend Carhart's self-propelled vehicle."[77] A prize of $10,000 was offered to any citizen of Wisconsin who could

> . . . produce a machine propelled by steam or other motive agent. . . . such machine to be cheap and practical as a substitute for horses, on highway or farm. That all machines entering the contest shall perform a journey of at least two hundred miles on a common road. . . .[78]

The course of the endurance race was laid out between Green Bay and Madison and the rules and supervision of the contest were to be determined by a special committee. Despite much preliminary advertising only two machines were ready at the appointed time of the race. The "Green Bay" and "Oshkosh," representing the towns of their origin, lumbered up to the starting line. The former was a large steam wagon with a horizontal boiler. Its driving mechanism was complicated by gearing which enabled the driver to change speeds according to the terrain. The latter was designed with a vertical boiler situated above the box heater. Two engine cylinders, one on each side, propelled the machine.[79] At the signal these huge wood burners were off to the cheers of thousands of spectators who had lined the route of the race. The "Oshkosh" finished the contest without mishap in 33 hours and 27 minutes, including stops for wood and water—an average speed of six miles per hour.[80] After several breakdowns the "Green Bay" dropped out of the race altogether. Considering the speed and performance of the winner the committee withheld the prize money because it believed the machine was not an economical replacement for horses. It was not until the legislature met some two months later that the owners of the "Oshkosh" were awarded $5,000.[81]

The Wisconsin race drew much interest throughout the nation prompting tinkers to improve upon the "Oshkosh." Engines were installed in buggies, farm wagons, velocipedes and bicycles. No one quite knew what design was best suited to carry their power plant and only a few were willing to change the traditional shape of the horsedrawn vehicle to achieve greater efficiency.

Of even greater interest is the fact that during the years 1880-1895, at the height of the steam age, experiments with steam vehicles declined. Only twenty-six patents for steamers were registered with the Patent Office in this period, compared to fifty-nine for gasoline-powered vehicles and an amazing forty-one for machines driven by spring motors.[82] Of course these are approximate figures and were changed by the many patents pending. To most inventors steam engines, consisting of steam, water, air and fuel systems which required constant attention were still complex. The major reason, however, for this change was the fear of fire and boiler explosions. In 1894, a spokesman for the factory inspectors of New York claimed that, "wherever steam power is used, danger is enhanced . . . and is frequently made more so by the carelessness, negligence or indifference of factory employees."[83] Four years later the factory inspectors reported that 39 per cent of the boilers used in factories were in a dangerous condition and submitted that, "this percentage of possible risks to human life and limb, from such a fearfully destructive force as boiler explosions is altogether too great to be allowed to pass without attention."[84]

People were also accustomed to reading frequent newspaper reports of steamboat disasters. In 1826, there were six steamboat explosions on the Hudson River and its tributaries.[85] One of the worst marine disasters occurred in 1840 and involved Commodore Vanderbilt's *Lexington*, the pride of the American steamboats. It caught fire from a faulty boiler and sank in Long Island Sound with a loss of 119 passengers.[86] Disasters such as these moved Congress in 1852 to strengthen existing steamboat laws by requiring all pilots and engineers to be licensed. Periodic inspection of all ships plying American waters was also required.[87] This action caused a decline in the number of sinkings, but the fear of an explosion still persisted. In spite of expert opinion that man was responsible, not the machine, the public believed the opposite. Commenting on the sinking of the palace steamer *New World* in 1855, an editorial stated:

> We doubt that in 99 cases out of a 100 a sufficient scrutiny would show that steam engine (disasters) are chargeable to gross carelessness or ignorance somewhere. A steam engine has not a will of its own. It cannot get up an explosion out of spite or perversity as a wilful horse runs away with the bits in its teeth. Men—are the ones at fault.[88]

The few marine diasters that occurred at the turn of the century still served to remind the public of the dangers of steam. The worst steamboat disaster of modern times took place on June 15, 1904, when the *General Slocum* caught fire and was gounded at Hells Gate, New York with 1,030 passengers losing their lives.[89]

The switch from steam to gasoline is best illustrated by the career of Ransom E. Olds. The son of a blacksmith turned machinist, young Olds was determined to build a horseless carriage. Using his father's Lansing, Michigan machine shop, he fulfilled his dream in 1886, producing a small but crude carriage.[90] A six-inch long gas pipe which was joined to several other pipes served as the boiler, while three stove burners produced a hot steady flame. Describing his experience with this machine and an improved model he recalled:

> I drove it out on River Street but it made so much noise that I had to run it between three and four in the morning in order to avoid scaring the horses. A few trips convinced me that there was no use trying to use steel gears and I decided to try to build

one using the ideas of a steam locomotive. I therefore made patterns for cylinders to go on each side of the carriage drive wheels, with a crank connected to each cylinder . . . the same as a locomotive. When completed in 1891, I found that a very high pressure was necessary to run it . . . even though fairly quiet . . . (it) could only be used on level roads.[91]

The Lansing *Journal* gave the vehicle a write-up which was noticed by the editor of the *Scientific American* who sent a reporter to verify the story. He in turn was impressed by the surrey's fifteen mile an hour speed and its ability to climb "ordinary grades."[92] He also noticed that the 1,200 pound machine was easy to operate since the steering lever and throttle were located by the driver's seat. In commenting on his creation Olds observed that

> it never kicks or bites, never tires out on long runs, and during hot weather he can ride fast enough to make a breeze without sweating the horse. It does not require care in the stable, and only eats while it is on the road, which is no more than one cent per mile.[93]

A one column article accompanied by an engraving subsequently appeared in the May 21, 1892 issue of the *Scientific American*. Shortly thereafter the Francis Times Company of London, a patent medicine firm, made Olds an undisclosed offer for the vehicle and, after some hesitation, the young inventor agreed to let his creation go for $400.[94] The vehicle was promptly shipped to the firm's Bombay, India office—the first instance of an American automobile being exported.

Olds' success indicated that steamers were saleable. Nevertheless, he realized that the drawbacks of steam far outweighed its advantages and decided to go with the internal combustion engine which, although new and untried, was safer and less complex.[95]

The gasoline engine was born in Europe and throughout the late nineteenth century no less than six experimenters laid claim to inventing it. Some point to the gasoline automobile invented in 1873 by Siegfried Marcus in Austria; others support the claim of Gottlieb Daimler, who drove a motor car in 1889 in Germany. The Automobile Club of France attests to Etienne Lenoir's horseless carriage built in 1862; but there is also strong evidence to bolster the claims of those who support the Germans, Nicholas Otto and Carl Benz.[96] In any event most of the internal combustion engines used during the sixties and seventies ran on coal gas and were used to supply power to small factories.[97]

In the United States there was little experimentation with the new form of power. Two engines which attracted much attention were the Brayton and the Langen-Otto. Both were single-acting types but differed in combustion and compression principles. The former was the creation of George Bailey Brayton, an Englishman who had recently emigrated to Boston. In 1871, he made a model engine which ran on either coal gas or liquid petroleum.[98] A short time later he was granted a patent on a non-exploding engine in which petroleum from a separate storage tank was vaporized, compressed and then forced into a cylinder where a small fire ignited it. The burning flame then heated the air which pushed the piston up and down.[99] The *Scientific American* of May 27, 1876 compared both engines, commenting that "The Otto . . . action is widely different. When the charge is fired beneath the piston, the latter . . . is shot upward with great velocity."[100] The Otto engine compressed an explosive mixture within the working cylinder, going through four cycles to achieve power.

Both engines left much to be desired even though the Brayton was quiet, smooth-running and similar in many respects to a steam engine.[101] The typical gasoline engine of the time was large, underpowered and needed heavy iron supports. Lenoir's engine, which first appeared in 1860, weighed more than a thousand pounds, yet it developed only a half horsepower.

By 1892, gasoline engines were limited to thirty horsepower or less and where larger engines were required they had to be made by joining several smaller ones. In most cases, large engines were difficult to start and small auxiliary engines were utilized for this purpose. To ignite the gasoline a tube-timer was employed: it was not always reliable.[102]

There was a clear difference between actual horsepower and rated horsepower. The *Scientific American* of November 26,

1892, reported that a hundred horsepower engine was in use at the grain elevator owned by the Taylor brothers of Camden, New Jersey. This engine was different: it dispensed with tube-timers, using instead a detonator which operated automatically after a hand-pump forced the charge into the cylinder. Running ten hours on a gallon of gasoline, which at the time cost only six cents, made it as economical as its steam counterparts. It also did not require the services of a fireman or skilled engineer. Nevertheless, the engine's real output was limited to only 62 horsepower, making it less powerful than a steam engine of similar size.[103]

The supremacy of steam power was now being challenged and modifications in engine design came from many quarters. To the talented inventor the main problem was to harness the internal combustion engine to a road vehicle; this required considerable time and money before any headway could be made. Describing his first experiments with the gasoline engine, the noted inventor Hiram Percy Maxim wrote that "it shook and trembled and rattled and clattered, spat oil, fire, smoke and smell and to a person who disliked machinery naturally, it was revolting."[104]

Maxim might also have added that it polluted the air. As early as 1895, he attempted to eliminate the noxious gases generated from this type of engine by adding a secondary combustion chamber, "wherein the exhaust gases are burned to their ultimate reduction," so as to "overcome the disagreeable odor of the exhaust of engines."[105]

Commenting upon the work with gasoline engines, the *New York Times* concluded:

> Horseless carriages operated by gas or gasoline engines are not a success at this time. Until the power is increased and the shaking reduced to an imperceptible amount, there is little probability of their being extensively adopted.[106]

The only other alternative to steam and gasoline engines was the newly developed electric motor, which was uncomplicated and simple to operate. The early electric carriages had four main components: an electric motor, a transmission gear, a circuit controller and a battery which stored up electricity and supplied current to the motor through the medium of a switch, while the transmission gear regulated the engine speed.[107] The electrics had many supporters but their disadvantages soon dampened the general enthusiasm. Equipped with one or two horsepower motors, they used their charge too rapidly and were therefore limited to between twenty and thirty miles a day. Recharging the battery took more than six hours.

In Europe where the automobile was no longer considered a novelty the situation was quite different. As early as 1894, a DeDion-Bouton steam drag finished first in the Paris-Rouen race of 79 miles, averaging 11.6 miles per hour.[108] A year later the public took notice of a Panhard gasoline car which won the 732 mile Paris-Bordeaux race with a speed of 15 m.p.h.[109] This contest proved that the gasoline engine was suited for automobiles and would be a formidable opponent for steamers and electrics. No one now doubted that the horseless carriage had come to stay. *The Motocycle* reported:

> In the thousands of vehicles that turn out in the Champs Elysees, the chief city driving avenue of Paris, the horseless carriage is now as one to five. They run noiselessly, swiftly, fascinatingly along the boulevards, and leave no doubt that the day of the horse will soon be done.[110]

"The growing needs of our civilization demand it," asserted the *Horseless Age* of 1895, "the public believe in it, and await with lively interest its practical application to the daily business of the world."[111]

In July of that year the editor of the *Chicago Times-Herald* offered $5,000 to the winner of a race for motor vehicles to take place in November on a course including the city of Chicago and its suburbs.[112] The results were surprising. Of the seven entrants who showed up on the day of the race, only two finished, and they did it with a gasoline-powered buggy. The winner, J. Frank Duryea of Springfield, Massachusetts, topped the field in his small vehicle equipped with a four-cycle gasoline engine. Despite freezing temperatures and recently fallen snow, he was able to cover the five-and-a-half mile course in seven hours and eighteen minutes. His average speed was about seven and a half miles per hour.[113]

No steamers had appeared at the starting line, although there were at least a dozen in the country capable of challenging the Duryea buggy. It must be remembered, however, that some twenty years earlier the steam-powered "Oshkosh" made a two hundred mile trip averaging six miles per hour. Undoubtedly the steam car's unpopularity was one good reason for its absence from this contest. The *Times-Herald* race and one held in New York City on Decoration Day, 1896, sponsored by *The Cosmopolitan Magazine*, drew Americans to horseless carriages. The supporters of steam now realized that an intense effort was necessary to overcome the challenge of the internal combustion engine. Between 1895 and 1900 backyard tinkers produced a multitude of machines which indicated that the steam car had been reborn.

The Stanley, Locomobile and White

The five years after the *Times-Herald* race were a time of considerable activity among inventors. In the words of the editor of *Motor World:* "There are not wanting indications that the first era of the automobile boom is nearing an end; . . . for the mechanical conveyance has come to stay, and the users are bound to increase in numbers."[1]

Both inventor and entrepreneur realized that the automobile could be the means to a quick fortune. Their problem, however, was complicated by not knowing what motive power would succeed and vehicles propelled by steam, gas and electricity had about the same number of supporters. In the race held at Narrangansett, Rhode Island in June, 1896 the Duryea brothers were beaten by Andrew Riker in an electric.[2] There were so many breakdowns, however, that the shout "get a horse" echoed continuously throughout the contest. It would soon become an epithet heard by all stalled motorists.[3]

Nevertheless there were a few willing to purchase these

horseless carriages. In 1896 Henry Ford sold a gasoline buggy to Charles Ainsley of Detroit for $200.[4] Two years later Elwood Haynes joined with the Apperson brothers to form an automobile company in Kokomo, Indiana.[5] At approximately the same time Albert Pope of Hartford, Connecticut, the nation's leading bicycle manufacturer, decided to enter the business; he favored the electric car. His Columbia surreys were advertised as spreading "the cause of safety, speed and simplicity in horseless locomotion over greater territory than any other make of vehicle."[6] By 1898 sixteen newcomers had entered the field and automobiles were now offered for sale to the public in quantity. A year later there were over a hundred hansom and coupe cabs in service in New York City; over ninety per cent of them were propelled by electricity.[7] At twelve miles per hour the electric cab could travel twenty to thirty miles on a charge, but recharging took more than six hours.

During this time many inventors made the small steam engine plant safer and less complex. In December, 1896 the Cruickshank Steam Engine Works of Providence, Rhode Island announced the sale of a steam truck to a local department store.[8] George W. Whitney, the enterprising marine engineer, had produced his fifth steam carriage and gave indication of building more.[9] Joseph Shaver's steamer attracted enough attention to receive a write up in the *Horseless Age*, while in remote Virginia City, Nevada, an interesting little carriage was built by W.E. Squier; it had a belt transmission and two engines, one for each wheel.[10]

It was during this period that the Stanley twins, Francis E. and Freeland O., originally school teachers in rural Maine, became interested in steam cars after seeing one at a country fair. Francis, the younger, had invested $500 of his savings in a photo gallery and within a few years operated three establishments in Lewiston. In 1889, he relocated to Newton, Massachusetts, where he operated a business making photographic dry plates from a new process he had discovered. Freeland later joined him in this venture which was so successful that it was bought by Eastman Kodak.[11]

Approximately nine years later the Stanleys decided to build an automobile and to make their task easier they purchased some of George Whitney's patents.[12] Not possessing the facilities to make a car of their own, the twins ordered the various components from independent contractors. The Mason Regulator Company of Milton built the engine, which weighed more than 400 pounds.[13] When completed, the 600 pound carriage, mounted on bicycle wheels, created a sensation during its first run through Newton.[14] It could "easily make twenty to twenty-five miles per hour on fair roads, up hill down dale." At a race held in Cambridge, the little carriage did a mile in two minutes and eleven seconds on a dirt track.[16]

News of the Stanley's success reached John Brisben Walker, editor of *The Cosmopolitan Magazine*, who called at the Stanley factory with the hope of selling them advertising. That the brothers did not believe in advertising mattered little to Walker,[17] who showed an interest in the car and ended up offering the twins $250,000 for their invention. After some hesitation they accepted and a new automobile company was formed.[18]

By the terms of the agreement, "the factory, its equipment . . . all cars and all patents and applications for patents pertaining to steam cars" were transferred to the new owners. The Stanleys agreed to refrain from making cars "for one year,"[19] beginning May 1, 1899. They would, however, continue to serve in an advisory capacity during this time.

With asphalt millionaire Amzi Barber, Walker formed the Automobile Company of America with its main office in New York City. In their first advertisement the new owners stated:

> The placing of the Stanley horseless carriage on the market opens up a new era. It brings within the reach of the man of ordinary means the power to travel in his own conveyance, at a rate of speed up to forty miles an hour . . . The purchase price involves an outlay of but $600.[20]

Within a few months Walker and Barber terminated their partnership, the former establishing the Mobile Company at Tarrytown, New York, while the latter set up the Locomobile Company of America at Bridgeport, Connecticut.[21] This division, coupled with the return of the Stanleys to the automobile business, was a serious blow to the development of the steam car as three major producers, each selling basically the same car, competed against each other against the manufacturers of gasoline and electric automobiles.

Walker soon found that it was more difficult to sell automobiles than magazines. He purchased the Philipse Manor property at Kingsland Point, near Tarrytown, New York, and erected there what was considered to be "the largest automobile factory in the world."[22] By July, 1900, his production figures totaled ninety carriages a week, but operation costs amounted to more than $250,000 per month.[23] This turn of events caused him to offer for sale $400,000 worth of preferred stock at a par value of a $100 per share.[24] Hoping his financial manipulations would save the company, he stepped up production and increased the number of models. Appealing to the safety-oriented buyer, the company claimed it had

> a horseless carriage weighing less than five hundred pounds and costing but six hundred and fifty dollars. Compactly built with workmanship of the highest quality, capable of twenty miles or more an hour. . . . it is operated by steam which renders it absolutely safe. More than a thousand Stanley carriages of the Massachusetts model are now in public use, and there has never been a single boiler accident. The fuel shuts off automatically when the steam reaches 160 pounds.[25]

Walker was particularly active in selling and promoting his product, and even coveted the commercial market by producing delivery wagons and omnibuses.[26] At the automobile show held at Madison Square Garden in November, 1900, the enterprising editor introduced a carriage designed for military use which, as the Boston *Transcript* stated,

> made the thirty-two miles to New York with three passengers aboard, in sixty-five minutes. It was exhibited on the track in the evening with four men in campaigning uniforms on the front and rear seats. It is a low, strongly built vehicle with a seat for two in front and a similar one behind, Between the two seats is a driving gear and large lockers for provisions, ammunition, tools and soldiers' kits.[27]

The Mobile was continually kept in the public eye. One ascended Pike's Peak to the timber line, covering the fifty miles without a breakdown.[28] Another swept to victory over five other steamers in a race held at Newport, Rhode Island in September, 1900, carrying off the Vanderbilt Cup.[29] Sales declined, however, and in 1903 the company went bankrupt.

During its brief life the Mobile Company produced 6,000 vehicles which included 21 models, ranging in price from the $550 carriage to the $3,000 heavy truck and limousine.[30] Price, however, was not the main reason for the company's failure. For three years Walker was selling the same vehicle that Amzi Barber and the Stanley brothers were selling. The competition among the three was too keen for the limited market and Walker became the first to find this out. During the same time, however, the Stanleys incorporated so many advances into their steamer that it became mechanically superior to the Locomobile and Mobile.

Amzi Barber's steam-powered Locomobile shared the same fate. Except for its name, the compact little carriage with its bicycle framework and light body was identical to the Mobile. Realizing this Barber tried to draw sales from the gasoline car by stressing the merits of steam power. An early advertisement declared, "Many people early last summer bought gasoline runabouts, but sold them later on to buy Locomobile steam cars. If you want a powerful and strongly constructed runabout, you cannot do better than to purchase a Locomobile. Silent in operation and easy to control."[31]

Starting and operating procedures were made to appear much simpler than they actually were. The 1900 brochure informed the driver:

> The operation of the Locomobile is extremely simple. The operator sits on the right hand side of the carriage with his left hand on the steering lever. With the right hand the throttle lever is pushed forward slowly. This admits steam to the cylinders and the carriage starts. The speed increases as the throttle lever is pushed farther forward. The carriage may be reversed as follows: shut off by bringing the throttle lever back to its initial position. Throw back

the reversing lever, and admit steam to the cylinders by the throttle lever.[32]

There can be no doubt that the early steam car brochures conjured happy dreams in the mind of the reader. Among those who expressed dissatisfaction with the vehicle was Rudyard Kipling. In a letter to the editor of *McClure's Magazine*, the famous writer said:

> . . . the Locomobile herself, she is at present a Holy Terror. If ever you meet Amzi Lorenzo Barber who I gather is President of the Company you may tell him that I yearn for his presence on the driving seat with me.
>
> I suppose she will settle down some day to her conception of duty but just now her record is one of eternal and continuous breakdown. She disgraced us on June 26th when I took two friends over 13 miles on a flat road. The pumps failed to lift and we had to pump dolefully every few miles home. Also she took to blowing through her platons.
>
> On June 29th we laid out a trip of 19 miles and back. I took the wife. She (the Loco) betrayed us fully twelve miles out— blew through her cylinders, leaked and laid down. . . .
>
> I tell you these things that you may think once or twice ere you get a Locomobile.
>
> It is quite true she is noiseless, but so is a corpse, and one does not get much fun out of a corpse.[33]

To offset unfavorable comments, companies often used testimonial letters, which they published in newpapers or incorporated into their brochures. Although exaggerated, such letters did serve to make a favorable impression on the public. Typical of the testimonials was that of Captain R.S. Walker of the Royal Engineers who was stationed in South Africa during the Boer War. In a letter to the company, dated August 10, 1901, the British officer declared:

> It . . . performed some very useful work in visiting outstations, where search lights were either installed or wanted, and in this way visited nearly all the larger towns in the Transvaal. It was responsible to go round all the likely places in one day, at every

station, which frequently meant considerably over fifty miles of most indifferent roads, more than a single horse could have expected to do—and the car generally carried two persons on such occasions.[34]

In another letter the City Surveyor of New York commented:

I purchased 50 gallons of stove gasoline at 10¢ and 8 gallons of stove gasoline at 15¢ per gallon. I also usd two quarts of cylinder oil and 1½ quarts of lubricating oil. These supplies were sufficient to run the "Locosurrey" a distance of 944 miles. Four passengers were carried, averaging over 165 pounds each in weight. There were no expenditures for repairs.[35]

The typical Locomobile was a well-built, silent, but complicated machine. There were more than twelve operations required to start the vehicle and failure to perform any one would render the machine useless. Among them were the filling of the water and fuel tanks, opening and closing a number of valves, pumping the air pressure to 35 pounds, heating the vaporizer tubes and starting the burner.[36] On the very early Locomobiles and Stanleys, the vaporizer was heated by a twenty-two inch long steel pipe called the firing iron. Heated red hot over a stove or furnace, it was carried with tongs to a small hole in the fire box where it was fitted into place. In many cases, though, the firing iron cooled before it could vaporize the gasoline and the driver had to repeat the heating process all over again.

Locomobiles required much attention and consumed large amounts of water and fuel. Water consumption was particularly great and conservative estimates indicate that the vehicle used a gallon for each mile driven. By comparison the manufacturer claimed that "it could be run on average roads for 40 miles with one tank of gasoline (14 gallons) and 20-25 miles on one tank of water (30-35 gallons)."[37]

Between the years 1900-1903 several new models were introduced, which were slightly larger and heavier. Boiler size on some models was increased to eighteen inches in length and more efficient pumps and accessories were added. In 1900, prices ranged from $700 for the "Stanhope" to $1,200 for the "Locosurrey."[38] A motorcycle, selling for $200 and billed as the "fastest pacing machine in the world," was also introduced that year.[39] Two years later a luxurious two-passenger vehicle, called the "Touring A" was placed on the market and cost $1,900.[40]

From 1900-1901, the company sold 600 cars a year in the United States and 400 cars in England.[41] The next year, however, sales declined and it was decided to manufacture gas cars. For three years the Locomobile Company had struggled against increasing competition, not only from other steamers, but also from the public fancy for gas and electric cars. At this time Andrew L. Riker, a pioneer in the development of electrics, designed a gas automobile along the lines of the French Panhard which attracted Barber. He was invited to join the Locomobile Company as chief engineer and the firm embarked on a policy of building luxurious gas cars in limited quantities.[42]

During this period the Stanley twins were quite busy. By December, 1899, only six months after the original agreement with Walker was made, the *Horseless Age* reported that they were building a steamer and in the fall of 1900 were ready to market it.[43] Called the "McKay," it was supposed to be protected under the patents of George Whitney which the Stanleys had acquired.[44] Amzi Barber became infuriated at the news of the "McKay" steamers being sold. He also learned that a turnbuckle used to adjust the chain was covered under the patents held by the Locomobile Company.[45] Accused of patent infringement, the Stanleys redesigned their vehicle by connecting a horizontal engine right to the rear axle, thus eliminating the need for a chain and the turnbuckle.[46] In April, 1901 the Stanley Motor Carriage Company was formed and production was underway by October of the same year. By this time the original agreement with Locomobile had expired and the twins bought back all their patents for $20,000. Thus within a two-year period the Stanleys reaped a quarter of a million dollar profit and were left with a large share of the steam car market.[47]

The new Stanley steamer had many refinements which made it an instant hit with the public. Since horsepower was determined by the size of the cylinder bore and piston stroke, the company offered buyers a Stephenson slide valve engine which came in three sizes: 3½ x 4½, 4 x 5 or 4½ x 6½. All engines were encased in sheet metal.[48]

Fire-tube boilers, which were redesigned and placed under the hood, came in sizes of 20, 23 and 26 inches respectively. The number of tubes increased in ratio to boiler size; the largest had 949 tubes which were 13 inches long and 33/64 inch in diameter.[49]

The Stanleys believed that a fire-tube boiler had a distinct advantage over other types because the tubes carried the fire and gases which heated the surrounding water. Firetube boilers had a greater heating surface and a greater steam storage capacity than other types. They were usually kept only two-thirds full, with the remaining space holding a reserve of steam. With so little water in the boiler, the water supply and burner flame had to respond automatically to increases and decreases in steam pressure. A superheating coil, situated directly over the burner, insured a flow of dry steam to the engine.[50]

All Stanley boilers were fitted with a fusible plug which was screwed into a steel fitting situated about three inches from the boiler's bottom. Should the plug melt, the driver would be alerted by hissing steam, which, if wet, indicated faulty circulation caused by dirt somewhere in the system. Dry steam indicated a low water level. The company advised that the plug be replaced once every three weeks.[51]

A small vaporizing type burner consisting of a pilot light and a main burner proved effective under most conditions. The pilot light was ignited when an acetylene or gasoline blow torch was applied to its vaporizer. On early Stanleys acetylene gas, called "Prest-O-Lite," was carried in a small tank on the running board and was an integral part of the car.[52] To many drivers this was real progress as it replaced the infernal firing iron of earlier models. By 1910, the company was able to substitute gasoline for kerosene as the pilot light fuel. In operation the fuel was forced by pressure through the vaporizing tube where, mixed with air, it became "thoroughly vaporized."[53] The main burner had its own vaporizer which was situated right over the pilot to keep it hot, and this enabled it to be easily ignited.

The Stanley was an immediate success and for the first few years the company had more orders than it could handle. Commenting on his product, Freeland said:

> My father and uncle were both firm nonbelievers in paid advertising. They belonged to that hardy yankee school that felt that if a product was good enough it could speak for itself much more convincingly through performance than any number of boastful words and phrases concocted by advertising men.[54]

In 1908 the company produced six models which included the Model EX Runabout, priced at $850, and the Model J limousine which cost $2,500.[55] Among the commercial vehicles made was an express wagon capable of hauling 2,500 pounds of freight, a light delivery wagon and a twelve passenger bus called a mountain wagon.[56] Several racers were also built which achieved national fame.

The mountain wagon was designed by F.O. Stanley to carry passengers from Loveland, Colorado to the resort at Estes Park, approximately thirty miles away. Equipped with the same power-plants as the Florida racers, namely a 26 inch boiler and an engine with a bore and stroke of 4½ x 6½, these vehicles were outstanding performers in rugged country. Before long they became popular at other resorts and among their users were the Hotel Wentworth at Portsmouth, New Hampshire and the Samosett at Rockland, Maine.[57] Mountain wagons were far more powerful than their gasoline counterparts and could negotiate any hill where they could gain traction. They were well suited for public transportation being free from vibration, noise and odor.

The name Stanley soon became a household word and the vehicles were always recognizable because of their rounded hood and silent operation. Almost all of them were painted Russian blue or royal green, except the "gentleman's speedy roadster," which was red with gold striping. The quality of workmanship was very high and only the best material was used. Bodies were made of aluminum and fittings were of brass, thus contributing to the long life of the vehicle.[58]

Sharing the spotlight with the Stanley was the White. The

history of the White Company can be traced back to New England where Thomas H. White and William L. Grout made sewing machines during the Civil War. After the war the partnership was dissolved and White moved west to Cleveland, Ohio where he continued his business. During the 1890's the company included in its operations the manufacture of lathes, screw machines, phonographs, bicycles and roller skates.[59]

In 1890 Thomas White's oldest son, Windsor T., a graduate of the Worcester Polytechnic Institute, became vice-president. Another son, Rollin H., joined the company upon his graduation from Cornell University where he had majored in mechanical engineering.[60] By 1900 Rollin had designed the company's first steam car, but it was not until April of the following year that one was sold. White cars met with the public's approval because of their efficiency and sturdiness and by the fall of 1901 production had increased to three cars a week.[61] Making steamers now took precedence over other manufacturing and Windsor White took charge of sales, Rollin assumed complete responsibility for production and design while the youngest son, Walter, became an assistant to his brothers.

The steam generating plant of the White distinguished it from other steamers of the period. In ordinary boilers water entered at the bottom and steam left through the top; in the White just the opposite occurred. Nine helical coils of steel tubing superimposed one above the other took the place of innumerable boiler tubes. These coils were joined in a series and if the entire unit were to be unwound it would consist of one, long piece of tubing.[62] There was no reservoir for the steam. According to Professor R.C. Carpenter of Cornell University, a member of the American Society of Mechanical Engineers, this boiler was a "continuous flow" type, generating only the amount of steam needed by the engine.[63] It could not be classified as a flash boiler because this type created steam as soon as the water came into contact with the hot metal.

Safety was the chief feature of the White boiler since there was little water and steam in the generator at any one time and in the event of a break in the tube, only an inconsequential amount of steam would escape. Professor Robert Thurston, Dean of the Cornell University School of Mechanical Engineering, said, "the tubular construction permits insurance of safety against pressures of excessive amount."[64] Professor Carpenter proved that the strength of the fittings at the point of leakage in the tubing varied from 7,000 to 18,000 pounds per square inch.[65] Normal working pressure for the system was 600 pounds.

The White engine was of the vertical compound type, common to railroad locomotives. Steam supplied direct from a generator was admitted to a small, high-pressure cylinder three inches in diameter and then forced into the low-pressure cylinder six inches in diameter.[66]

A water regulator of the diaphram type was designed to alternately direct water toward the generator or divert it from the water pumps, according to whether the steam pressure was above or below the normal working pressure of 600 pounds.[67]

Rollin White, in an effort to conserve water, designed an efficient condenser which was cooled not only by flowing air induced by the motion of the car, but also by a fan. The latter, though, added to the car's complexity since it was driven by a chain-drive from the crankshaft which in turn was connected to a shaft and ball-bearing arrangement.[68]

Most steamers underwent design changes and the White was no exception. Except for the boiler and engine, a number of modifications were made during the first two years of production. In the 1906 White brochure, the company said:

> To see the little White Stanhope of 1901 side by side with one of the Model F cars one would hardly imagine that the two machines had anything in common. A critical examination, however, would reveal the fact that the mechanism of the one represents a logical and constant evolution from that of the other. The generators and automatic devices in the two cars, the most vital features, except for the difference in capacity, could almost be regarded as interchangeable.[69]

As with most steamers of the period, starting the White required some technical knowledge and great patience. The company claimed they could furnish the car, but "the driver must furnish the brains."[70] Instruction booklets contained detailed instructions and numerous warnings. The 1903 brochure stated:

> The knowledge of the car is not acquired in an hour, nor in a day, each part should be taken up separately, until thoroughly understood. Do not make the great mistake of driving fast until you have become familiar with the working parts and operation of the car under all conditions of the road.[71]

Similar in many respects to other steamers, the White had a sub-burner which had to be ignited first. Then began the laborious process of hand-pumping the air, water and lubricating pressures. A number of valves had to be opened or closed during this procedure.[72] The instruction booklet advised that once the steam pressure had risen to 400 pounds, the driver should proceed slowly for the first mile since it took that distance to heat the engine and generator. The driver who was in a hurry was advised "Do not get the idea that you must run at full speed all the time. It shortens the life of your car and you may shorten other lives."[73]

During the years it produced steam cars the company endeavored to produce as many different models as possible. Among them was an open five passenger touring car called the "elephant" steamer and the Model G, which came with a touring, limousine or pullman body. The pullman body could seat seven and featured two revolving chairs which enabled passengers to enter and leave without any discomfort.[74] The Model G, equipped with a pullman body, cost $3,700. It had a 115 inch wheelbase, was fourteen feet in length, and weighed, with a full tank of water and fuel, only 2,433 pounds.[75] With its standard 30 horsepower engine it was more than a match for its internal combustion powered competition. After 1902 the cheapest White cost $2,000, yet more than 700 cars a year were sold.[76]

In an effort to increase sales the company decided to manufacture commercial vehicles, and by 1903 White trucks, buses, ambulances and patrol wagons were in demand everywhere. Particularly helpful to sales was a report submitted by the United

States Army to the Quartermaster-General which stated that the White

> is simple in operation. The means of propulsion being steam. It is better suited to the transportation of the sick and wounded than gasoline cars on account of its smooth and free running, freedom from violent vibration and ease of controlling the speed between maximum and minimum without jerks or jolts.[77]

The above report was favorably received and in 1905 the United States government purchased its first self-propelled ambulance, a White steamer.[78] Additional orders followed and the Navy Department, not to be outdone, also purchased White ambulances.

Although records listing the exact number of ambulances sold are missing, it is known that the White was the first choice of many hospitals. Recognizing the advantage of steam power, the Superintendent of Philadelphia's Public Health and Charities Department stated:

> The first ambulance was delivered to us in November, 1906, and was put in charge of a man who had been driving one of our horse ambulances, thus proving your claim that the "White" system for simplicity and control is without equal in automobile construction . . . The ambulance will do the work of four horse-drawn vehicles and we are able to save the lives of patients by getting them within reach of medical assistance rapidly. We have yet to experience any stoppage on the road due to mechanical difficulties.[79]

The Superintendent of the Department of Public Charities for New York City said:

> The White steamer has many qualities which cause it to be particularly adapted to ambulance service. Prominent among them is the absence of jolting, the ability to go long distances without recharging and the lack of necessity for cranking the machine.[80]

Orders for Whites poured in from all over the world. The City of Rio de Janeiro, Brazil purchased three patrol wagons specially equipped to carry fifteen prisoners.[81] In 1906 the Dutch government ordered five commercial vehicles equipped with special bodies for carrying the mails in the remote regions of Java.[82] In the same year the Jidosha Company of Osaka, Japan bought nine steamers for its bus line. It was in England, however, that the White obtained a stronger following than in any other foreign country. A branch was established in London as early as 1901 and sales reached 200 cars yearly.[83]

Much of the company's sales success was due to the favorable publicity their cars received from racing activities and from their users, particularly the government. During the San Francisco earthquake of 1906, the White received national recognition when it was used for rescue work.[84] The city of San Francisco, with its innumerable steep hills, posed a problem for electric and gasoline-powered vehicles. Horse-drawn wagons could negotiate the steep grades only with great difficulty. Thus the disaster of 1906 proved to be more serious than indicated because many automobiles lacked the power to undertake rescue work. In a letter to the company Mrs. G.A. Hawkins, wife of the manager of the San Francisco White branch, said:

> The garage in San Francisco is burned. Automobiles were saved. . . . We have a machine and a chaffeur here who will go back to Oakland as soon as necessary. Gasoline is scarce, and oils. . . . All automobiles and wagons possible are taken for military purposes. Your automobiles were in use constantly so long as the gasoline permitted, carrying dead and wounded and dynamite.[85]

Walter White, then in Los Angeles, heard of the calamity and drove his steamer to the burning city, offering his help to the army.[86] His call for more steamers was quickly answered and the work of saving the injured was undertaken immediately. Hundreds were evacuated in a few days while precious supplies were transferred to various points in the city. All of this was done efficiently and rapidly because of the steam car's ability to climb steep hills and work day after day without a breakdown. This was an amazing feat which earned the praise of many.[87] The rare photograph collection showing the White steamers during this emergency which still exists is an important record of the automobile's role in a changing world.[88]

The Locomobile, Stanley and White took the lead in producing steam cars but by 1911 only the Stanley survived. That year the White company switched to gasoline cars because public reception for them was at an all time high. The official company statement on the change was:

> Although the White Company was building more large touring cars than any other make they discerned a marked improvement in gas engine design in Europe and realized that further development of the gas car would present a vehicle superior to one operated by steam.[89]

The passing of the White meant not only the loss of a major producer of steamers, but also the loss of a leading pioneer in steam car research. Many companies attempted to compete with the gas car but few had the life span of the White and Stanley.

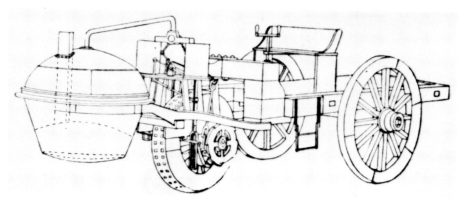

1. Nicholas Cugnot's three-wheel steam artillery carriage, 1769, with details of the single flue boiler and driving connections.

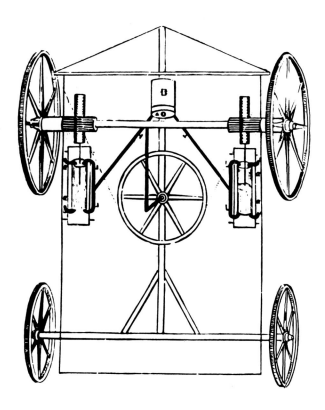

2. The Nathan Read carriage, circa 1790.

3. Oliver Evans' "Orukter Amphibolis," 1804.

4. Walter Hancock's "Automaton," circa 1836.

5. The Lane brothers, *left to right*, David, William and John.

6. The Lane Roadster, Model 8.

7. The Stanley twins.

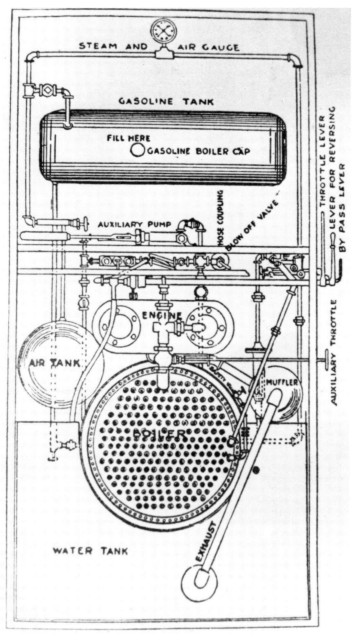

8. A plan arrangement of the Stanley
"Locomobile" carriage.

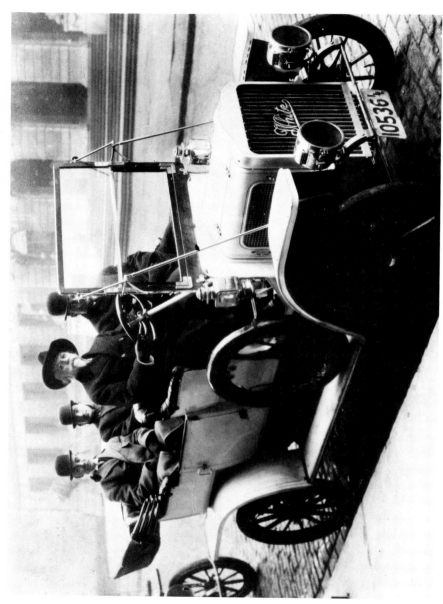

9. William F. "Buffalo Bill" Cody in his Model O
White steamer in 1908.

10. The right side of the White steam engine, with the side plate removed from the crankcase to show the valve guide.

11. "Whistling Billy," the White racer.

12. The record-breaking Stanley racer, 1906.

Greatest Hill Climbers ever produced as shown by tests in the Alleghany Mountains.

Baldwin

NO VISIBLE
EXHAUST

(Steam) Automobile

PERFECT
INDESTRUCTIBLE
BURNER

BALDWIN
AUTOMOBILE
MFG. CO.

CONNELLSVILLE, PENNA.

13. An advertisement for the Baldwin steam car.

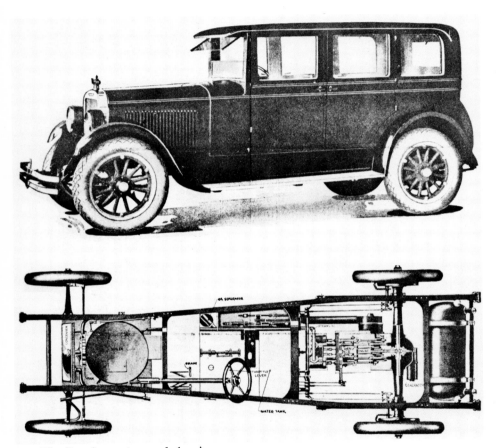

14. The Brooks steamer and chassis.

15. The Doble E-11 five-passenger touring car, 1924.

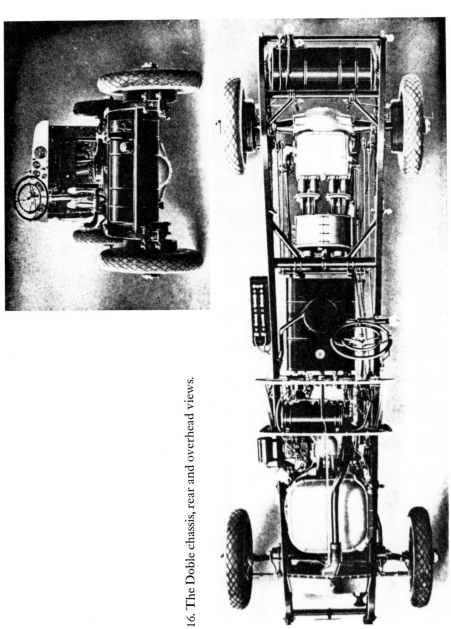

16. The Doble chassis, rear and overhead views.

17. The Williams brothers' roadster.

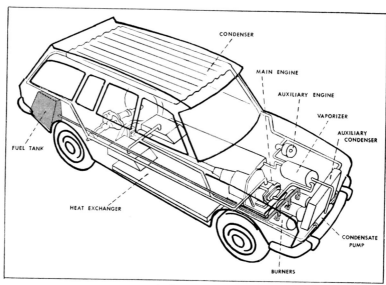

18. A diagram of Wallace Minto's fumeless car.

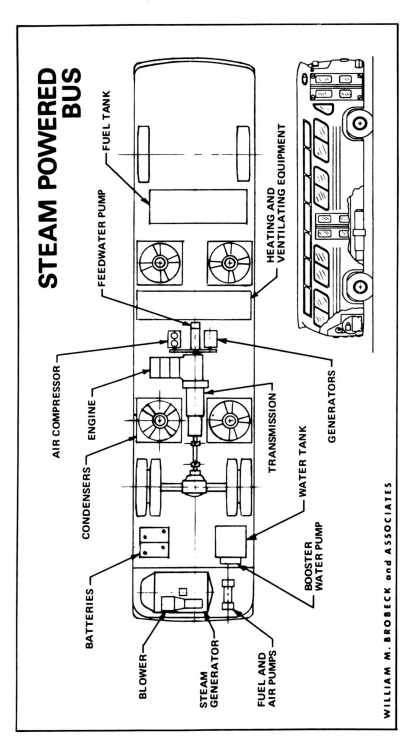

STEAM POWERED BUS

FUEL TANK

FEEDWATER PUMP

HEATING AND VENTILATING EQUIPMENT

AIR COMPRESSOR

ENGINE

CONDENSERS

TRANSMISSION

GENERATORS

WATER TANK

BOOSTER WATER PUMP

BATTERIES

BLOWER

STEAM GENERATOR

FUEL AND AIR PUMPS

WILLIAM M. BROBECK and ASSOCIATES

19. Layout of the components in the William Brobeck & Associates demonstration bus.

20. The Lear Vapordyne racer, an experimental vehicle which has never been run.

21. The Lear steam unit installed in a Chevrolet Monte Carlo. The vapor generator (indicated by white circles) has been removed to expose interior parts.

IV

One Hundred and
Thirty-four Others

The March, 1909 issue of *Motor* magazine lists 639 firms that had built or were building automobiles.[1] Of course this list is not complete because many new companies were born after that date—but it does indicate that building automobiles was a major industry at the time. Eventually there were almost 2,900 makes of cars; this was made possible by the fact that a comparatively small sum of money was needed to enter the business and by the many investors who had faith in the automobile.[2]

My search of trade journals, collections and newspapers has turned up the names of approximately 137 companies or individuals which had built steam cars. Many of these firms made gas or electric cars along with steamers. According to one source the Kensington Company of Buffalo, New York took no chances and made steam, gas and electric cars, but was in business less than four years.[3] The companies that made steamers were short-lived. Most of their sales were local and, lacking sufficient capital to advertise or improve their product, they soon found their markets exhausted. Two small firms which proved these laws of survival inapplicable to them were Grout and Lane.

In 1882, John G. Lane and his three sons William, John and David, moved to Poughkeepsie, New York from nearby Millbrook where he had established his coffee mill business.[4] Within a few years the business was expanded to include door-hangers, various mechanical devices and scientific instruments, probably the largest variety of items made by any one firm in the country at the time.[5] It was soon clear that William was the inventive genius of the family and within a few years he was granted patents on a hayrake, a self-measuring faucet and a water motor for sewing machines.[6]

In 1889, William built his first car—a small two passenger buggy which attracted much local attention. Other cars followed and by 1900 the Lane Motor Vehicle Company was an established enterprise. In many respects the new car was not a typical steamer. The boiler, for instance, was divided into two parts; the top half being of the fire-tube type where water was partly changed to steam. The conversion process was completed in the bottom half which was of the flash type. All boilers featured fusible plugs.[7]

In 1903 the company changed to the compound engine, believing it to be more efficient than the conventional double-acting type. Placed obliquely below the body in order to lessen vibration and shorten the chain length to the rear axle, it was readily accessible for service. According to the 1903 brochure:

> The whole engine below the cylinder is enclosed in a copper oil case, and the motion of the engine splashes oil over all the parts. The piston rods and valve stems also carry sufficiently into the interior, and additional oiling of the cylinders is seldom if ever required. Under these conditions, viz, protected from dirt and thoroughly oiled, wear is infinitesimal.[8]

Of particular interest was the Lane burner, made up entirely of tubing. The mixing tube protruded through the center of the device which "insured a uniform mixture of air and vapor."[9]

Straight rows of flame were fed by an air current which provided a uniform supply for all driving conditions.

Despite the efficient burner Lane owners had to follow the same starting procedures as other steam car enthusiasts. The only exception being that on the Lane one ignited the vaporizing tubes of the main burner with an alcohol lamp instead of a torch. The instruction book advised that the driver should "use his judgment in setting the valve for continuous feeding of the burner and in no case allow any liquid and but very little if any gasoline to enter the burner since a rich flame will be suffocated." [10]

After the flame was raised an automatic regulator shut off the burner, but the pilot remained lit. The water indicator was then adjusted and a warmed-up engine drove out any water in the cylinders. The driver then opened the "forced draft valve," placed one foot on the brake, and with the other, moved the forward and reverse levers ahead. The throttle was then opened and closed two times and the reverse lever thrown back; steam was now admitted. [11] Thus, after fifteen minutes of preparations, the car was ready for operation.

Eleanor Lane Taylor vivdly recalls her experiences with the family cars. In a letter to her cousin she wrote:

> I think that about thirty miles an hour was as fast as we ever went; for years the speed limit was twenty and the roads of those days supplied their own speed control. . . . I do recall that as a small child, probably around 1900, we would spend three days getting from Poughkeepsie to my grandfather's place outside Philadelphia and in the summers three days driving from Poughkeepsie to Ogunquit, Maine. I remember that there was frequent condemnation of the noisiness of gas engines and that steam cars were very quiet . . . One of the most vivid memories of touring is of looking for water to fill up the boiler—it was siphoned in from horse troughs or from streams along the way. One of the nice things to do was to take friends for a Sunday afternoon drive of the thirty mile circuit down around the base of Storm King Mountain and it did take all afternoon. [12]

The Lane was a well-built and mechanically sound

automobile which was much simpler to start and operate than other steamers. Raising the air pressure needed to force fuel to the burner was completely automatic, being accomplished by steam pumps which worked off the engine. The company stressed automatic features in its advertising:

> A carriage may be operated indefinitely without hand pumping of any kind. The operation of getting up steam has been simplifed to the manipulation of one valve, and the vehicle will stand indefinitely under steam, ready to move at any moment. The boiler pressure will remain constant and the safety valve will not blow off.[13]

A widely promoted feature was the automatic by-pass valve, which eliminated hand pumping to obtain proper water level in the boiler. Selling for only $15, it was not adopted by other manufacturers.[14]

Although the vehicle was widely advertised in the automobile trade journals, the company never sold more than twelve cars a year during its ten year existence.[15] A total of 22 different models were built and each year the cars were increased in size until the 1910 Lane rested on a ten foot five inch wheelbase. Of course each car was hand built of the finest materials obtainable. The bodies were of aluminum, the frames steel and the fittings of brass. The weight varied from 2,350 pounds for the touring car to 3,100 pounds for the large tonneau. Priced at slightly more than a dollar a pound, the former sold for $2,650 and the latter for $3,400.[16]

The Grout Brothers Automobile Company of Orange, Massachusetts gave every indication of taking a large share of the early auto market. Originally manufacturers of the "New Home" sewing machines, the company, founded by William L. Grout in 1859, had built a reputation for making quality products. By 1885, William could boast of making one sewing machine for each working minute of the day in his company's modern factory where 125 men were employed.[17] Much of the company's early success can be attributed to efficient management. To the few that can still remember the Grouts it is known that when "the whistle blew at 7:00 a.m. the shop gate was locked and if anyone came in a minute late, they had to go through the offices to get their job . . . and Grout would be there to give them a sharp call-down."[18]

It was in this finely equipped factory that William Grout's two sons, Charles and Frederick, received their training. It was Frederick, however, who emerged as a mechanical wizard and he devoted much of his time to automobiles. In 1896, he built a gasoline buggy, but became dissatisfied with the necessity for changing gears, the noise and the smell of internal combustion engines. Two years later he was operating a steam wagon on the streets of Orange and his experiments led him to conclude that only steam vehicles could be improved to the point where they could be successfully marketed.[19]

Impressed by his son's experiments William altered the factory to produce automobiles. By 1900 more than 200 Grouts were made and all signs indicated that he had made the right decision. The typical Grout had a two-cylinder double-acting engine of the Stephenson link slide-valve type, completely enclosed in an aluminum case. All cars were built in the finest traditions of the New England craftsman and were described by one reporter as

> being a beautiful example of small motor design and finishing. The cylinders of the Grout engines are cast together with a steam-chest between them, the vertical D-valves moving horizontally and sliding on their lower edges to avoid coasting wear. The cylinders are bored with bars on a thoroughly good single spindle horizontal boring mill, and are practical duplicates. The pistons have each four rings, two in a pair, one outside and one inside, both eccentrically bored, pairs pinned together so as to give 4-100-inch more thickness opposite the flat surface laps . . . The piston rods are bronze, the engine frames are bronze.[20]

The heart of the Grout was its fire-tube boiler, which came in 18 or 20 inch sizes. Designed with 530 copper tubes, 16 inches long and a ½ inch in diameter and surrounded by a 5/16 inch-thick steel shell, it was guaranteed to be explosion proof.[21]

The cast iron burner was slotted and had an airmixing adjustment to permit proper combustion. The pilot light was situated directly in front and was controlled by its own hand-wheel and valve. Both were less efficient than the types found on the Stanley, and had a tendency to go out or flare up if not properly adjusted or if dirt accumulated in the slots.[22]

In most respects Grouts were typical steamers, differing only in style. Between 1902-05, most Grouts were designed with a barrel-shaped hood flanked by two huge headlamps. Some models had only one of the huge "solars" located in front of the hood giving the vehicle the appearance of a giant Cyclops. Bodies were of aluminum, mounted on wooden frames and came in either carmine or merrimac green. Later models came equipped with a 43-gallon water tank and a 15 gallon fuel tank, an advantage on long trips since the Grout had no condenser. Total weight of the car, including full water and fuel tanks, was 1,750 pounds.[23]

At the height of the steam car's popularity, the company offered several models including the $900 "New Home" steam coupe which appealed to physicians and a $950 "dropfront" touring car. The cheapest and most popular model offered was the $650 runabout.[24] By 1905, however, declining sales forced the company to reduce the number of models and only the runabout and a $1500 "side-door" tonneau were made. A model called the "Weston" was sold in England, but this did little to increase profits.

An attempt to save the company by building a gasoline car failed to bring the desired results. The new car had a thirty horsepower, four cylinder engine mounted in a wooden chassis but, since financial difficulties had seriously curtailed production, few were made. By 1909 the company was in the hands of the receivers and Grout became another name on the list of failures.

Steam still had many supporters although its popularity was declining rapidly. Before 1910 the distribution of companies was national, with Massachusetts leading all other states with eighteen firms: New York had fourteen, Pennsylvania seven and Ohio four. Steamers were also built in Nevada, California, Washington, D.C. and in thirteen other states.

New York State was a leading producer of automobiles during the first decade of the twentieth century. Between 1899 and 1905 some fourteen companies produced steamers, while numerous others turned out gas buggies and electrics. Several firms, besides Lane, were already well-known by 1900 and the state was second to Massachusetts in the number of cars produced.

Among the early leaders was the Foster Automobile Company of Rochester, New York. In 1900, the firm exhibited its first models at the Madison Square Garden Bicycle and Automobile show, which prompted the *New York Tribune* to state that

> the popular interest exhibited in automobiles at the Madison Square Garden Bicycle and Automobile show during the last week was in a large measure concentrated on the motor carriages made by Foster and Company, a firm of Rochester manufacturers. The vehicles manufactured by this firm are noteworthy for their simplicity and mechanical construction and the excellence of their workmanship. They combine all the features calculated to appeal to anyone interested in a light pleasure carriage . . . Those who . . . may be interested to learn that the Foster machine was conceded by many experts to be far ahead of anything of that description on the market.[25]

The car received much favorable publicity from its victories in hill climbs and endurance runs. In September, 1901 the company entered a six horsepower, 1,350 pound touring wagon in the New York to Buffalo Endurance Run, and it was able to outlast most of the other entries.[26] This was no easy feat as treacherous roads and steep grades took a heavy toll of vehicles of all types and weights.[27]

Fosters came in only three models, whose prices rose as sales fell. The 1900 carriage weighed only 650 pounds and cost $650; at a dollar a pound many considered it quite a bargain.[28] The same carriage cost $1,000 in 1903, and this price did not include a condenser, mud guards, double-acting bulb brake side lamps and tools, all of which cost $200 more.[29] With sales continually declining the directors sold out to the Artzberger Automobile Company of Allegheny, Pennsylvania, but within two years this firm also folded.[30]

Strong competition from the Stearns steamer probably

caused the Foster Company to fail. Built at Syracuse, only ninety miles from Rochester, it was designed by Edward C. Stearns, a former Canadian bicycle manufacturer. Conventional in all respects, the steamer came equipped with a two-cylinder, eight horsepower engine.[31]

Much of the company's early sales success was no doubt due to the nine models it offered: a $600 runabout, a $1,200 delivery wagon, a $750 buggy with a victoria top and a $1,200 four-passenger surrey.[32] Commenting on its policies, the company said:

> The opportunity for improvement on the prevailing types of steam carriages being offered induced the Stearns Steam Carriage Company to place upon the market a carriage built upon more substantial lines than the lighter types, and without the ponderous appearance of some of the road machines of the day. The carriages marketed by this company have universal satisfaction; and also have given the Stearns carriages a conspicuous place among the leading automobiles of the day.[33]

Limited to 200 vehicles a year, sales declined until in 1903 the company went bankrupt.

The story of Foster and Stearns is typical of that of the firms which made steamers in New York. None achieved any marked success and only a few were able to attract capital for research and advertising. Other firms which failed were: Century, Conrad, Twombly, Kensington, Rochester, Wood-Loco, and Elite. Because of the steam car's poor image they could not possibly have been successful in the limited steamer market which declined each year. Foster competed with the Rochester Cycle Company in the same city. This was also the case with Stearns and Century. These four companies, less than a hundred miles apart, without a large scale organization and without reserve funds, had to fail in an industry with a high attrition rate.

The same situation existed in Massachusetts, then the nation's leading producer of automobiles of all types. It was here that the Duryea brothers built the first successful gasoline automobile and the Stanleys the first saleable steamer. Colonel Albert Pope, an early automobile pioneer and president of the

Electric Vehicle Company, originally began his enterprise in Boston and the Grout brothers claimed to have built the first automobile factory in the nation at Orange in 1896. In 1905, the city of Springfield had five companies in its midst and could lay claim to being the center of the automobile industry.[34]

The area in general was excellent for the automobile industry to grow in: it had good rail service, cheap labor and a tradition of industrial knowhow. In 1905 eighteen firms there were engaged in the business of making automobiles, but within five years only two had survived.

The Overman Bicycle Company of Chicopee Falls was among the first to enter the business when in 1899 it introduced a two-passenger carriage priced at $850.[35] Called the Victor, it possessed features which made repair a mechanic's nightmare. The "Bullard-automatic boiler feed system," for instance, could not be understood or adjusted without constant reference to the owner's manual.[36] An automatic fuel cut-off also added to the driver's miseries. The company was quick to point out:

> Every Victor is carefully tested and adjusted before leaving the factory, and it is strongly advised that the adjustment not be changed or tampered with. In case of any difficulty with the carriage, or if any part should break, a full description of the injury and its occurrence should be sent . . . at once to one of the company's factories, and, if possible, the injured or broken part itself should be sent . . . It is felt that to insure perfect results, the operator himself should co-ordinate the directions set down with the results of his own experience and good judgment.[37]

Each car came with a cylindrical fire-tube boiler capable of creating 200 pounds pressure in ten minutes. A fusible plug safeguarded the boiler. The two cylinder, verticle engine of four horsepower propelled the car at speeds up to 25 miles per hour.[38] The 1903 carriage weighed 1,150 pounds and came equipped with two five gallon gasoline tanks and "enough water for 22 to 25 miles."[39] Only two models were made and these were in the $1,200 to $1,400 price range. A decision to produce gas cars prolonged the company's life until 1904, when it was decided to sell out to the Stevens-Duryea Company.[40]

Daniel Brownell and Charles B. Edwards also hoped to corner some part of the automobile market with their small steamer. These Taunton businessmen started operations with $200,000 in stocks and considerable optimism. According to the local newspaper:

> The officers of the new company are very confident that everything is auspicious for good work in this line just now and it's certain that the people of the city wish them every success in their undertaking. [41]

The Taunton steam carriage came with a three-cylinder engine which had a bore and stroke of 2¾ x 3 inches. The entire unit was enclosed in an aluminum case and geared directly to the rear axle by bevel wheels. A water-tube boiler with a superheating coil supplied the steam. [42]

Carrying 40 gallons of water and 20 of gasoline, the Taunton weighed 1,200 pounds and cost $850. [43] It was tillersteered and had two extra seats situated under the dashboard. The company operated from 1901 to 1904 and judging from the size of the factory probably did not produce more than thirty cars a year.

In New England the Stanley Motor Carriage Company was the leading producer of steam cars and the Pope Manufacturing Company, later the Electric Vehicle Company, the giant of gasoline and electric cars. A small firm with limited capital could not have challenged these big concerns and survived. Even the Locke Regulator Company of Salem, a long time manufacturer of regulators, pump governors, and valves stopped competing after only four years. Its Puritan steam car was competitive in price, rakish in design and featured a fold-away steering wheel and a foot-controlled throttle. [44] These features certainly made it competitive with the Stanley, but did little to increase sales. Without adequate capital for research and advertising, the Locke Company could do nothing but go out of business.

It was during this period that New England lost its grip on the automobile industry. In Detroit, Ransom E. Olds and Henry Ford, advocates of cheap automobiles, found the capital to produce gas cars. On the other hand, New England's Albert

Pope had suffered a severe setback. His Electric Vehicle Company, whose grand resources "stood at more than $100,000,000," all of it on paper, was near failure after its attempt to promote electrics.[45] New England, it appears lost to Detroit because of inadequate leadership. According to John B. Rae

> it comes down to a matter of men, with due allowance for the influence of economic and geographic forces, Detroit became the capital of the automotive kingdom because it happened to possess a unique group of individuals with both business and technical ability who became interested in the possibilities of the motor vehicle.[46]

Builders of steam cars could do little to alter this situation since they were no longer in contention by 1903. During this period sales of Stanleys remained constant. The public, it appeared, was still willing to buy the car because of its outstanding performance and simple steam plant. Non-condensing engines and firetube boilers, although less efficient than condensing compound engines, were more attractive to a driver who lacked technical knowledge. The Stanleys could have easily adopted the flash boiler which was a great time saver. Pioneered in 1888, by Leon Serpollet, the French engineer, the multi-tube flash boiler could raise steam in a matter of minutes, and it was economical since it generated as much steam as was immediately required.[47]

It was also known that Stanleys had an insatiable thirst for water, but the twins would not adopt a condenser or anything else that would complicate their car. Only when a sixteen-year-old genius named Abner Doble showed them the advantages of condensers did they add radiators and fans to their cars in 1915.[48]

The Stanleys were also the only successful builders of automobiles who rejected advertising. Without this medium they could never dispel the myths associated with steamers. Fires and boiler explosions, for example, were held by the public to be risks all steam car owners had to accept. An early pioneer in advertising stated:

> When we make specific and definite claims, when we state actual
> figures or facts, we indicate weighed and measured expressions.
> We are telling either the truth or a lie. People do not expect big
> concerns to lie. They know we cannot tell a lie in the best medi-
> ums. [49]

The Stanleys never sought outside help for research or expansion
and never considered a merger. A combination of White and
Stanley would certainly have given Henry Ford, William Durant
and the Dodge brothers something to think about.

Unfortunately a combination of steam car manufacturers
never materialized. Even White failed in an attempt to license
manufacturers to build its cars. [50] Thus competition rather than
merger or licensing proved to be the rule among builders of
steamers.

In the Great Lakes region the White Sewing Machine
Company was challenged by the formidable American Bicycle
Company of Toledo, Ohio. Stressing economy, simplicity and
sturdiness for its steamer, the company showed a small carriage in
the fall of 1900 which it called the Toledo. [51] Within a year it
was ready to market a four ton steam truck, an electric car called
the Waverly and five types of steamers. [52] Occupying the largest
booth at the second annual Madison Square Garden Automobile
Show, the firm boasted:

> If you are looking for a moderate priced motor car with ample
> power, that is easily understood, easily controlled, that costs little
> to maintain and operate, and that, at the same time has style,
> by all means get a Toledo steamer. [53]

Reporters for the *Horseless Age* said the cars were easy to ma-
nipulate on city streets and also were "one of the heaviest constructed vehicles on the market." [54] Toledos had already received
recognition when in October, 1901 five carriages traveled the 63
miles from Toledo to Detroit in two and three-quarter hours without a breakdown. [55] At approximately the same time a Model A,
weighing 950 pounds, made the trip from the factory to the
New York Auto Show completing the 900 miles in fourteen
days without mechanical problems. [56] This particular feat is
noteworthy because few gas cars and certainly no electrics were

capable of the same performance. Quality control at the factory was one good reason for the car's success in these endurance runs. Before delivery "each Toledo was inspected as carefully as a government rifle," and rejected parts were "consigned to the scrap heap."[57]

The company attempted to crash the low-priced car market with its $600 Model A carriage which was equipped with a four-cylinder compound engine, a water-tube boiler and a bunsen type burner.[58] Other models, distinguishable primarily by body styles, cost as much as $1,600.[59] Sales declined, however, and in 1903 the firm sold out to the International Motor Car Company. That same year it exhibited only one steamer and four gas cars at the Madison Square Garden Automobile Show.[60] For three years the Toledo was widely advertised and was a strong competitor because of its low price. Unlike the White, though, most of the cars were sold in the Great Lakes region, and when this market was exhausted the company was in trouble. Acquiring agents in the large cities did little to increase sales.

Another Ohio firm which collapsed after much fanfare was the Geneva Automobile Manufacturing Company of Geneva, Ohio. The entire venture was conceived by James A. Carter, a local bicycle builder who acquired the patents of James Thompson in 1901.[61] Backed by Cleveland money, Carter made his first steamer that same year and exhibited it at the Pan-American Exposition in Buffalo, New York. The ambitious inventor believed that steam would be the motive power selected by the buying public and planned to build a hundred cars by April of the following year. Extensive renovations were made in his plant, a former cycle factory, and many believed the new company would become a major industry in the region.[62] Much of the optimism which followed the firm's debut was probably due to an article in the *Horseless Age* which said:

> In the body, the conventional dash of the horsedrawn vehicle is done away with and the front end is so constructed that there is ample room in it for the air and gasoline tanks and tools, thus removing the gasoline tanks from the proximity to the fire. By putting a back rail and a cushion on the front an extra seat is furnished.[63]

The car's water-tube boiler was seventeen inches in diameter and seventeen inches high with a "crown sheet" riveted in nine inches from the top, which left "a suitable water chamber." A six horsepower two-cylinder engine of the marine type propelled the vehicle. The company claimed that the forty gallon water tank was sufficient for 30 to 50 miles, while the 15 gallon gasoline tank gave a cruising range of from 100-150 miles.[64]

Four models, each upholstered in high-grade leather, ranged in price from $750 to $1,750. Despite the claim that it was "the most luxuriant two-passenger steam car made," the company was unable to attract enough customers to stay in business.[65] The competition was particularly tough since the White factory was only forty miles away and the Toledo plant 170 miles away, and this prompted Carter and his stockholders to build gasoline cars. The decision, however, came too late and the company failed in 1904.

The year 1904 was significant for the Ohio steam car manufacturer as up to this time six firms had failed in the attempt to produce a marketable steamer, among them: Gaeth, Aultman, Cincinnati, Hoffman and Stringer. The Hoffman, for example, was produced by a Cleveland bicycle company which also made gasoline cars. Selling steamers and gas cars at the same time, though, did not help, and the firm closed its doors in 1904.[66]

Any discussion of steam cars must include the Pennsylvania automobile industry. At least ten companies were in business during the first decade of the twentieth century and all of them failed by 1906. The city of Reading, a major rail and industrial center, seemed to be the likely place to build automobiles. It was here that Irvin Lengel, backed by New York capital, organized the Steam Vehicle Company of America, with the intention of building a steamer of his own design.[67] Called the Reading, the small carriage had a four-cylinder vertical engine rated at 5¾ horsepower and a water-tube boiler tested to withstand 700 pounds pressure.[68] The water tank held 32 gallons and the gasoline tank eight gallons, enabling the car to travel nine hours without a refill. Readings were competitively priced between $750 and $1,150, and were advertised as "a practical machine which can be safely operated."[69] Few cars were sold, though, and the company went into bankruptcy in 1902.[70]

Lenzel, however, was determined to build a saleable steamer, and with backing from E. W. Alexander, president of the Alexander Hat Company, formed the Meteor Engineering Company.[71] After some minor alterations to the factory sixty men were hired and production was begun on both the Reading and Meteor, the former a lower-priced companion to the luxurious Meteor, which came equipped with a four-cylinder ten horsepower engine. A water-tube boiler with a working pressure of 200 pounds generated the steam. The 1,600 pound Meteor carried 45 gallons of water and 20 gallons of gasoline, sufficient amounts for a fifty-mile trip.[72] Advertised as being built along "the French gasoline lines," Meteors came in three models ranging in price from $800 to $2,000.[73] Hoping to increase sales, the company exhibited two of its cars at the New York Auto Show at Madison Square Garden and despite the fact that thousands of prospective customers attended the event, not one of them ordered a Meteor.[74]

At approximately the same time, the firm received an order for 100 cars from a Philadelphia distributor, but the contract specified only gasoline engines, something the company could not produce. As a result of these developments it was decided to dissolve the Meteor Engineering Company in the fall of 1903.

A similar story can be told of the Baldwin Automobile Company of Connellsville. In 1900, the stockholders of the Slaymaker-Barry Lock Company decided to enter the automobile business with a light, speedy steam carriage. The factory was completely renovated and the latest equipment purchased to produce all components for the steamer, except the wheels, tires and bodies.[75] According to a contemporary account, "the main building consisted of a machine shop and erecting rooms, 400 feet by 40 feet, with an addition 200 feet by 30 feet." Included in the structure was a complete iron and brass foundry and a hammer shop. At the beginning of production several hundred men were employed at one time.[76]

The company turned out only one model, a light runabout

equipped with a two-cylinder engine of the Stephenson slide-valve type. A condenser was mounted in front under the dash. An advertisement appearing in the *Motor Age* of July 26, 1900, claimed the vehicles to be "the greatest hill climbers ever produced as shown by tests in the Alleghany Mountains."[77] This boast, however, did little to increase sales. By December, 1900, after only five and a half months of operation, the Baldwin Automobile Company was in trouble.[78] Before the spring of 1901 the company had shut down after producing no more than 200 cars.

Elsewhere the situation was the same. The Boss Knitting Machine Works of Reading, in business from 1903 to 1907, also gambled with steam. An early company advertisement boasted that "Steam is the only reliable power in the world."[79] Boss steamers came equipped with a two-cylinder, eight horsepower engine and a seventeen inch water-tube boiler. The entire steam generating plant, however, was situated under the driver's seat, a design that was already outmoded. As a result few buyers could be found who were courageous enough to sit over a roaring fire. Selling hand-built cars, though, did keep the company in business for three years. According to a report in the *Cycle and Automobile Trade Journal* "seventeen coats of paint and varnish give an enduring polish, and upholstery of the best leather adds to the general elegance of the car."[80]

Even at little Meadville (population 12,000) two steamers were built, by the most unlikely mechanics. George Randall, a conductor for the Erie Railroad, finished his car in 1904, and although it attracted much local attention, nothing was ever heard of him or his machine again.[81] A year later Andrew Watson, a paperhanger, operated his car down the main street, but after several breakdowns gave up his automobile venture.[82]

Only a few attempts to build cars throughout the nation met with success. Most firms built automobiles as a sideline and only a few dared to give up their diversification. The important factors were: location, leadership, available capital, design and of course public preference. In 1900, the trend was toward steam, with 1,681 steamers being sold as compared to 1,575 electrics and 936 gas cars.[83] By 1902, however, sales of gas cars shot upward and within two years steamers were outdistanced.

The movement away from steam becomes clear when one looks at the official government figures:

		1909	1904
Number of establishments		316	168
Machines			
	Number	127,289	22,830
	Value	$165,115,100	$24,630,400
Gas			
	Number	121,274	19,837
	Value	$155,068,100	$20,446,100
Electric			
	Number	3,639	1,425
	Value	$6,564,500	$2,469,300
Steam			
	Number	2,376	1,158
	Value	$3,482,500	$1,688,000[84]

It has been generally accepted that the reason for the sudden increase in gas car sales was the marketing of a popularly priced car by Henry Ford and Ransom E. Olds. This is not so. In 1908, the Model N Ford sold for $600 F.O.B. Detroit and certainly proved popular with the public.[85] Olds' curved dash runabout was also a big favorite, and it was purchased by more than 4,000 buyers at $650.[86] Both Ford and Olds proved that production in quantity and low price were important factors for success. The evidence, however, shows that steam car manufacturers were the first to sell low priced cars, as indicated in the table on pages 80 and 81. Most steamers sold for less than $750; the $550 Mobile and the $450 Wood were the lowest priced vehicles available on the American market. Both appeared at approximately the same time as the popularly priced gas cars, yet were rejected by the buying public.

The reason for the downfall of the steamer must lie with its image of that time and with the public's fear of boiler explosion and fire which, as previously stated, were common. In December, 1899, many boiler inspectors were demanding a full engineer's license for operators of steam carriages.[87] Five years later certain steam cars were excluded from coverage by the major insurance companies because of the fire hazard.[88] In fact many sales were lost when a flooded burner caused the fire to creep through the floorboards and singe a prospective buyer's trousers. Sales naturally declined because little was done to dispel the fear of fire and explosion.

PRICES OF STEAM AND GAS VEHICLES, 1897-1905

STEAM

Year	Make	Price
1897	Stanley carriage	$700
1900	Tractobile (Pennsylvania Steam Vehicle)	$625
1900	Porter Stanhope	$750
1900	Leach No. 2	$600
1901	Mobile Runabout	$550
1901	Reading Model C	$850
1901	Rochester	$750
1902	Wood (Wood Vapor Vehicle)	$450
1902	Stanley Model C Surrey	$750
1903	Locomobile dos-a-dos	$650
1903	Locomobile Runabout	$950
1903	Grout Model H	$750
1903	Whitney (Brunswick, Maine)	$800
1903	Conrad Model 70	$800
1903	Toledo Carriage	$800
1903	Reading Model H	$1,150
1903	Stearns Model D (without top)	$600
1903	White Steam Stanhope	$1,200
1904	Grout (with detachable top)	$650
1904	Foster Touring	$650
1905	Boss (with top)	$1,000
1905	Stanley Model E Runabout	$850
1905	Lane Touring	$2,250
1905	Clark Tonneau	$5,000

GASOLINE

1897	Winton	$1,000
1901	Winton Touring	$2,000
1901	Starin	$800
1902	Olds (curved dash)	$650

	Make	Price
1902	Olds (curved dash with top)	$750
1902	Peerless	$2,200
1903	Buick	$1,250
1903	Ford Model A	$850
1903	Overland (Standard Wheel Co.)	$595
1903	Franklin	$1,300
1903	Haynes-Apperson	$1,800
1903	Rambler Runabout	$750
1903	Jones-Corbin (runabout)	$1,000
1904	Crestmobile	$750
1904	Packard Model L	$3,000
1904	Maxwell	$750
1905	Franklin (runabout)	$1,400
1905	Cadillac Model B	$900
1905	Studebaker (rear entrance)	$1,250
1905	Wayne (Model C)	$1,250

Bankers, always on the alert for a sound investment, naturally turned their back on a car which did not have a favorable public image. Without capital, the builders of steam cars could not improve their product and therefore lost the technological race with the gas car. One economist has claimed that:

> there have been relatively so many automobile failures is, however, upon second thought not so surprising. One would expect the hazards to be greater in a new industry, especially one making a complex fabricated product, subject to constant change and improvement in design and construction. This recurrent necessity of making innovations both in the character of the product and in the methods of manufacture . . . probably serves to explain in large measure the complete disappearance of many names that were once highly respected.[89]

By 1902, bankers recognized that purchasing automobiles was good for business and when this happened the new industry went on a solid footing. Many automobile securities were sold and lending operations by local banks became common.[90] It also became apparent that bankers had faith in the less complex and fireless gas car which always seemed to be improving. The internal combustion engine was new and held much hope of being perfected. On the other hand, steamers changed little from year to year and could not overcome their unfavorable image. Even a banker who knew little of engines realized that the internal combustion engine was explosion-proof and therefore felt it was at most a "safe" gamble.

Builders of steamers could do little to alter this situation and accordingly failed. Nevertheless, the steam car, although it lost ground rapidly, still managed to survive to 1910 because it was a better performer. The motoring public knew well the power and accomplishments of steam on the nation's roads and for this reason alone they were still willing to buy the car.

V

The Fastest Cars in the World

The life and death struggle between steam and gas cars attracted the attention of the entire nation. President Theodore Roosevelt purchased a White as the official White House car and bolstered the spirits of steam car enthusiasts.[1] Taking full advantage of the reliability of steam power, Roosevelt had decided that he would not be embarrassed by the gas car's stalling, noise or noxious fumes.

His successor, William Howard Taft, continued the steam car tradition and this prompted the editors of the *White Bulletin* to comment:

> While in Washington, the President uses his White car in going about the city, and while he was spending his vacation at Beverly, a long ride in the country was part of his daily routine. In addition to the President's personal car, two White steamers were used during his stay at Beverly by the Secret Service officials in the discharge of their highly important duties.[2]

The preference shown for the White in government circles

was by no means confined to the executive. As previously noted, the War and Navy Departments adopted White ambulances; then in August, 1909, the former, under direct orders from Major-General Leonard Wood, Commander of the Department of the East, purchased five touring cars to be used in military maneuvers.[3] Once again one must point to the recognized dependability of steam over gasoline power under all conditions and over all types of terrain. According to General Wood:

> The White steamer which I used during the maneuvers rendered most satisfactory service, without a breakdown or delay of any kind. The average running of the car was about 150 miles per day, over all kinds of roads and under various conditions of weather, which gave it the severest kind of test. . . . The opinion of all who saw enough of the car to form an opinion was that it is a most excellent car and reliable machine and one well-fitted to render good service under the harshest conditions.[4]

Other high-ranking officers agreed with their commander's judgment of the White, all of which served to establish beyond a doubt that the gas car was still a primitive machine, which could not be trusted to perform under battlefield conditions.

This decision was made in 1909, and not one member of the Association of Licensed Automobile Manufacturers, an organization of 34 producers of gasoline cars who recognized the validity of the Selden patent, could boast of having their vehicles adopted by an official government agency. Such prominent names as Stearns, Thomas, Franklin, Pope-Hartford, and Cadillac all failed in competition with the steam car.[5] In fact the White Company consistently maintained that an automobile should perform well wherever it went. R. H. Johnson, New York representative of the firm, proved this point by promoting tours throughout the country and his efforts focused attention on the need for good roads.[6] The company was also among the first to establish a touring bureau which distributed booklets giving detailed road directions. Eventually many motorists drove on trails originally blazed by Whites.[7]

Steam-powered automobiles were also popular among doctors who found them useful for making house calls. In response to a request by the editor of the *Horseless Age*, doctors reported their experiences with automobiles of all types. To Dr. J. G. Henry, a steam car seemed an economical and practical substitute for the horse. Costing $600 and equipped with $180 worth of accessories, the little steamer served the doctor well for four years.[8] During this time it broke down only twice, but Dr. Henry claimed the first breakdown was due to his own neglect because he failed to tighten a connection linking a piston with the crosshead. He said:

> I have found it a great time saver, especially on long trips. My long rides in the hot summer are never irksome, but always enjoyable, and I feel just as certain of getting to my destination on time as when travelling by rail, and very seldom is this confidence misplaced. . . . After four years of hard service this car looks like new and runs as smoothly as ever and so far as I can judge all vital parts are in excellent condition.[9]

It cost Dr. Henry three cents a mile to operate his car which made 15,000 miles. Total expenses were $489.65 of which $278.38 went for tire repair and replacement and $207.52 for gasoline. Oil costs were only $3.75.[10] The entire cost of operation was limited to essentials; not one cent went for parts and labor. This was probably due to the care the doctor gave the car and the slow rate of wear associated with steam engines.

Dr. E. C. Chase, a New Hampshire physician, favored the gasoline car, in spite of its noisy operation and periodic backfiring. He claimed that he never had any difficulty negotiating steep hills and found the vehicle well-suited for his practice. Nevertheless cost of operation was high, amounting to five cents a mile—but it was still cheaper than horses.[11]

Electricity proved the least popular motive power. One doctor, who preferred to remain anonymous, said:

> The most disturbing feature in operating an electric car is the time consumed in charging, an hour's run taking two hours to replace, sometimes more. In my own case the annoyance is reduced to a minimum by an individual charging plant, my power being supplied at a flat rate of $10 a month. Every time I reach home I connect to the charging plant and aim to start out with a full

charge. The whole cost of running the car for ten months in a year . . . has not exceeded $185. My monthly mileage is about 250 miles. This makes the total cost per mile about 7 cents.[12]

There was certainly no unanimity of opinion as to which of the power agents was best because all were expensive and all had drawbacks.

Until 1910, automobiles were unperfected machines which gave their users a certain amount of trouble. Engineering improvements were few, except in the case of the internal combustion engine which seemed to change yearly. After much debate manufacturers adopted the four-cycle motor as the standard of the industry because it had superior balance and kept the power effect constant. In such an engine there are four stages (intake, compression, ignition and exhaust) which characterize the cycle. Taking two revolutions of the engine to complete, it was claimed this caused an "irregular driving effort, making large flywheels necessary if the main shaft is to rotate uniformly."[13]

In the two-cycle engine these four stages are carried out in one revolution of the flywheel and without the benefit of poppet valves, push-rods and camshafts. Although much simpler in design, such engines could not attain high speeds, turning only 400 revolutions per minute as compared with the 1,500 revolutions of the four-cycle type.[14] When the four-cycle internal combustion motor is fully charged with gasoline and air, it is doing all the work it possibly can. The amount of work it does during each power stroke is thus definitely limited. The rate at which the engine does its work, i.e., its horsepower, is directly proportional to its speed; its maximum torque or pulling power is roughly constant when taking its full charge. The Association of Licensed Automobile Manufacturers figured horsepower by squaring the bore, multiplying by the number of cylinders and dividing by two and a half. This formula was widely used until the development of the high compression engine.[15]

The internal combustion engine, however, had just so much usable power. In a gas car which proceeds up a steep hill the engine is required to drive the car at the speed it is moving.

As the grade increases and the power required is constantly increased the engine and car slow down because the engine cannot develop enough energy to propel the vehicle's drive wheels. Of course if the grade increases sharply the engine and car will stop. Thus the importance of a transmission in early gas cars cannot be underestimated. If the engine speed or r.p.m.s is increased by changing gears, more power will be transmitted to the drive wheels and the car will be better able to negotiate a steep grade.

In a steam car power is stored in a boiler and released when necessary. A steam generator and engine would be working at between 900-950 r.p.m.s when the car's speed was 60 m.p.h.[16] At this number of r.p.m.s the gas car will stall. A typical Stanley could sustain a steady speed of 45 miles per hour without lowering the boiler pressure and had the potential of a "breathtaking sprint for a mile or so if required."[17]

Of course durability and strength of components were also important in determining a car's worth. Steamers were constantly plagued by defective pumps, clogged burners and leaking gaskets. One frequent problem was the scaling and incrustation in the boiler tubes caused by the presence of impurities and insoluble salts (mainly calcium carbonate) in the water. Although a nuisance it was usually corrected by "blowing off" the boiler two or three times a week. In this operation the car was stopped and the steam released under pressure through a tube and valve situated under the boiler. According to the *Steam Motor Journal*, "if this matter of blowing off is properly attended to the boiler can be run continuously on very hard water with no injurious scaling or deposit."[18] Internal combustion cars appeared to have as many if not more problems. Manufacturers believed they could alleviate much of the trouble by cutting weight. Albert L. Clough, a noted authority on automobiles, said:

> . . . fuel efficiency and durability both become subsidiary to light-
> ness in the minds of the designers and up to a certain point,
> this position is warranted in the present state of the art, as styles
> and practice in automobiles change so rapidly that a machine is
> generally discarded before it can wear out, making it a course

of doubtful expediency to construct a long-lived motor, especially at the sacrifice of some other more valuable quality.[19]

At the time tire and wheel failures were the most common cause of breakdown. During the first ten years that cars were sold in quantity wheels were usually made of wood, the artillery type proving to be the most popular. Under strain, however, the wooden spokes came loose, causing the spoke support to weaken, thus making the wheel useless. Wire wheels, so popular with bicycle manufacturers, were not practical on automobiles because "side stresses" caused them to buckle.[20] Very few favored tubular steel wheels because they had little elasticity and were prone to distortion. Disc wheels, composed of nothing more than two circular steel plates, were the strongest, lightest and least expensive wheel one could buy.[21] Despite their inability to give a spring effect, they were widely adopted.

The greatest trouble, however, came from blowouts. An early attempt to eliminate punctures by using hard rubber tires was unsuccessful because they produced a hard ride and unbearable vibration.[22] The only other alternative was the pneumatic clincher tire which became standard equipment on automobiles at an early date. These tires, of the type used on bicycles, were unsuited for large cars as they made tire-changing a difficult task. Every motorist dreaded the experience of forcing his big tire over the clincher rim. This problem was partially overcome by the straight-sided tire pioneered by Firestone and Goodyear. In 1907, a Goodyear advertisement boasted that a tire change took one minute with their "universal and detachable tires."[23]

To prevent blowouts, punctures and rim cuts early drivers looked to protective coverings and during this time hundreds of patents were issued for cure-all devices and outer protectors. Leather covers proved quite popular for a time and one company made its entire casing out of the material.[24] The placing of steel plates or fine chains between the rubber and the canvas proved impractical because the steel wore through after extended use. It was not until stronger tire fabrics were developed, however, that the motorist's lot was made easier.

Significant developments did occur in braking but the accident rate from faulty brakes was still high. The very first cars were equipped with primitive shoe brakes which acted on the periphery of the tire, but they had limited stopping power and distorted the tire.[25] It was not long before engineers developed the internal expanding brake now found on modern automobiles. On a few cars an auxiliary transmission brake was added, consisting of a drum and lining mounted on either the drive shaft of a gear-driven car or on the sprocket of a chain-driven vehicle.

Of course a brake was only as good as its lining and for many years various substances were used to reduce heat and friction. Vulcanized fiber, leather and asbestos proved popular but some motorists preferred camel's hair belting because of its superior heat resistance and its performance in the presence of oil and water.[26] With such improvements as these the speed and power of automobiles could be increased with less chance of accident.

Performance was of course an important consideration in selecting an automobile and racing and endurance runs became the means by which a manufacturer could discover faults in his product. Until 1897, fifteen miles per hour was the average speed for motor cars until a Panhard hit almost twenty-four miles per hour in the 106 miles race between Paris and Dieppe.[27] The Panhard continued to make records as it did in 1898 when it won the 1,440-mile Tour de France averaging 32 miles per hour. Two years later a sixteen-horsepower Panhard established a record of 36.6 miles per hour, but lost the hill-climbing contest to a twelve-horsepower Mors.[28]

There can be no doubt that European racing had a big impact on the fledgling American auto industry. The *Times-Herald* and Rhode Island races proved that racing was as popular as any sporting event. Several manufacturers exploited the public's interest in speed by taking their vehicles on long distance trips. In 1897, Alexander Winton made a 700-mile journey from Cleveland to New York in 40 days at an average speed of 6½ miles per hour.[29] The feat received much publicity since a reporter accompanied Winton for the entire distance.[30]

By 1901 endurance runs and circuit racing had become common in urban areas where the wealthy congregated. On April

26 the Long Island Automobile Club held a 100-mile endurance run which started and ended in Jamaica. Sixty-one cars entered the contest, but only thirty-seven finished. Except in the case of the Whites, the run really proved nothing since the rules were slack and the breakdowns numerous.[31] The *Motor World* stated:

> If the event turned up any sensation it certainly was in the performance of those sensational vehicles the White steam carriages. Two of the vehicles went through without a stop or skid of any kind. The third stopped only because the terrific wind that prevailed there extinguished its pilot light.[32]

Shortly after this fiasco the club decided on a run from New York to Buffalo to be held in September. Of the 80 vehicles registered for the event, 54 had internal combustion engines and 26 were steam-powered; there were no electrics. Everything began well, but when the cars got as far as Rochester the run stopped because of the assassination of President McKinley.[33]

The efforts of the participants, however, did not prove to be a complete waste; many vehicles had participated in the Nelson Hill Climb, near Tarrytown, during the first step of the contest. Cars were segregated according to weight and in the Class A event for vehicles not exceeding 1,000 pounds, a Grout came in first and a Locomobile second. The Grout was able to cover the 2,300 foot course in two minutes and forty-five seconds.[34] A class B event for vehicles weighing between 1,200 and 2,000 pounds was won by a gasoline propelled Autocar in three minutes and seventeen seconds. A Locomobile came in second only thirty-eight seconds behind and a Stearns steamer took third in four minutes and two seconds.[35] No steamers were entered in the Class C event which was for vehicles weighing more than 2,000 pounds.

Hill-climbing events and endurance runs were one means of eliminating newcomers to the industry who had little to offer. The reliability run was particularly important: it afforded the manufacturer an opportunity to test his stock product and improve the design of component parts. On the other hand road or speedway racing put the entire car through a rigorous test of its ability to attain high speed. To this end many cars were streamlined and made lighter and sturdier. Of particular importance was the car's motor which had to withstand the high r.p.m.s without a breakage.

It took only a few years for high-speed racing to develop into a popular sport for both spectator and participant. The dangers involved, however, caused the editor of the *Horseless Age* to say:

> . . . Road racing in the United States is a breach of the common law, an excess dangerous to the participants as well as to the ordinary users of the highway, a temporary fad at best, and a diversion of the attention of the public from the more useful and enduring branches of the industry. Under no circumstances can interest in the sport be long maintained because the limit of the speed possible on roads must soon be reached.[36]

The most popular position, however, was stated by the automobile enthusiast H. Ward Leonard in a talk before the Long Island Automobile Club:

> The chief cause for the existence of the modern automobile is speed. There are few persons who want a slow automobile after having ridden in a moderately fast one. A touring car should be capable of making from 30 to 35 miles per hour on a first class level road. The almost universal figure given as the speed of the light touring cars of the French makers is 50 kilometers or about 31 miles per hour.[37]

Of course local authorities would decide just how fast a car could go. Although speed laws varied from city to city, twenty m.p.h. was the most the law would allow. In New York City it was 15 m.p.h. on the public streets and 25 m.p.h. in the under-developed areas.[38]

By 1902 racing fever had swept the nation and automakers welcomed the opportunity to demonstrate the superiority of their cars. An early test of vehicle speed and efficiency was sponsored by the Automobile Club of America at Staten Island in May, 1902. This event, however, provided more information about economy of operation than anything else. Light steam carriages, for example, consumed gasoline at the rate of one gallon every 6 2/3 miles. Water consumption was seven times as great. Internal combustion-propelled carriages of the same weight got 17 miles to the gallon.[39] The only steamer which came close to this figure was the White, which got 12.8 miles to the gallon.[40] The steam car's poor showing in this category was due to the inability of the steam plant to convert heat effectively into mechanical energy. The gasoline used to raise steam in the burner gave a large part of its heat to the surrounding air through chimney gases and radiation from the boiler and this proved wasteful.[41] The problem, however, was overcome by substituting the much cheaper kerosene for gasoline which reduced costs for steam car enthusiasts.[42]

Among the speed contests which attracted wide attention was the Detroit Race Meet held on October 11, 1901. The White Company entered its little stanhope, equipped with a stream-lined body and new flash boiler. To the amazement of the crowd, it hit 30 m.p.h. and swept to victory in the five- and ten-mile races.[43] A year later the same vehicle carried off all honors at the Cleveland, Ohio race meet, covering a five-mile course in six minutes and forty-four seconds. It also won the five-and ten-mile steam car races and took first place in the ten-mile handicap.[44] These successes were repeated on the west coast and served to strengthen the image of the White, and of all other steamers.

In 1903 a White equipped with a compound engine and tonneau body and driven by Frank Garbutt, competed in the May 9th and 10th Los Angeles Race Meet.[45] According to the *White Bulletin:*

> In the first race of the day, two miles for cars of 1,500 pounds and under, (he) shied a little at the turns and the best he did was to finish second to another White car driven by Walter Grothe. But the experience he gained in the initial contest was of great value to him later. In the next race, the five-mile-free-for-all, Mr. Garbutt's performance was remarkable. Not only did he beat the large gasoline machines . . . but he also established a new record for the distance and drove the fourth mile in faster time than

an automobile had ever travelled west of the Mississippi. In the three mile race he again finished in front of the other contestants.[46]

Garbutt and his White were now feared in racing circles and in the next few months he added to his reputation by winning several more events in California. Among his achievements was the run from Del Monte to Oakland in four hours and thirty-three minutes, establishing a record which gas cars failed to match for many months.[47]

The English Reliability Trials of 1903 served to enhance the reputation of steamers abroad. In this event cars were required to travel 1,019 miles and participate in hill-climbs and speed tests. The results once again showed steam to be superior. Two Whites finished in the first division and one of them made seven non-stop runs. During the race a White travelled at between 38-58 m.p.h. with a full load of equipment and passengers, a feat unmatched by gas cars.[48] By 1906 the Automobile Club of Great Britain had banned steamers from all competitive events allegedly because such cars could raise considerable steam while idle and "thus a 10 horsepower nominal engine could develop 30 to 40 horsepower say for a brief spurt and make nonsense of the classifications."[49] This argument, like many others used against steamers, is not quite accurate because the White had a "continuous flow" boiler which generated steam quite rapidly.

In the United States steamers were not popular either. Many entry blanks for races contained the words "For Gasoline Cars Only" in spite of the fact that these races were open to cars of a certain price as listed in the company's catalogue.[50] There were also many cases of participants owning gas cars who withdrew from a race in which steamers participated. On one occasion Whites were banned from the Wilkes-Barre race held in the summer of 1907. To prevent a protest the racing committee claimed that the steamers were left out of the contest to create openings for gas cars. Actually the committee realized the futility of permitting gas cars to compete against steamers after Walter White, driving a Model G, won the hill-climbing contest.[51]

During the summer of 1903 two White racers called the "White Turtle" and "White Snail" made their appearance at mid-western tracks with astounding success, winning medals and first class certificates. It was at this time that company driver Webb Jay and his 15 horsepower White became the talk of the racing world. On August 28, 1904 he took three first prizes at the World's Fair races held at St. Louis.[52] This speed event was particularly noteworthy because Jay's White defeated a French Panhard, a Peerless and a Pope-Hartford, all rated at 24 horsepower, in the five mile race. In the ten-mile contest the White came in second to a sixty horsepower Pope-Toledo but managed to finish ahead of four other gas cars whose motors were rated at 24 horsepower.[53] Jay continued his spectacular victories, matching or surpassing the performance of any gasoline car built in the United States or abroad.

After the Pittsburgh race meet held on September 30, and October 1, 1904 the *Automobile* magazine reported:

> Webb Jay defeated a field of seven starters in the five mile for cars up to 16 h.p., with road equipment in 8:35. Pitted against him were E. Haas in Al Banker's Pierce, W. N. Murray in a Franklin, J. A. Pietsch in a Stevens-Duryea, H.A. Martin in a Pope-Toledo. . . . Webb Jay also won the two mile event for cars up to 16 h.p. with road equipment. He drove a White and finished in 3:35, with George Stranahan second in a Franklin. . . . The same victorious steamer driven by Jay, captured a two mile race for cars up to 24 horsepower in 2:46. Turner in a Peerless ran second.[54]

At the Cleveland Race Meet on October 15 Jay once again proved the superiority of steam over gas. His little White took first place three times and swept the five-mile open handicap, defeating the highly regarded Winton Bullet III, an eight-cylinder racing car.[55]

The little White racers continued their success all through the next year, astounding the automobile world. They even competed in the annual hill-climb held at Eagle Rock, New Jersey, which attracted every major auto-maker in the world. Among those represented was a ninety-horsepower gas car specially built for speed and many high-priced foreign cars. Although the White racer "Whistling Billy" finished fifth, it was still a victory of sorts because it was the best showing by an American machine. According to the Brooklyn *Daily Eagle:*

> The most noteworthy performance of the contest was the 1 minute 23/25 seconds record, the fifth best time, made by Webb Jay in a 15 horsepower White steamer. This little American car which is not a racing machine, but practically a stripped down touring car, selling at $2,500, climbed the hill in only 3 3/5 seconds slower time than the big foreign cars costing $16,000 and having over four times the horsepower.[56]

The string of victories piled up by Whites indicated to the motoring public that steam was a mighty challenger. The White, among the fastest cars of the day, also had excellent braking power and won the first important braking trials held in this country, an event supervised by the United States Department of Agriculture. The trials, held on Long Island in May, 1909, proved that the White was from 38-45 per cent more efficient than its nearest rival. The official government figures showed that at 20 m.p.h. the steamer took 31 feet to stop, at 30 m.p.h. only 74 feet and at 40 m.p.h. 140 feet. [57]

Stanleys also won many victories at the time. In fact they had been setting records from the time they were introduced to the public before the turn of the century. As early as August 31, 1899, a little runabout conquered Mount Washington; it took three years for a gas car to duplicate this feat.[58] In 1904 F.E. Stanley, driving a Model EX, went up the same trail in 27 minutes flat, establishing another record.[59]

Improved Stanleys led to more triumphs. On May 30, 1903 a crowd estimated at from 12,000 to 15,000 people jammed into the Readeville Trotting Track at Hyde Park, Massachusetts to see a number of speed contests sponsored by the Massachusetts Automobile Club. Many makes of cars were represented and race officials felt that "it would be too dangerous to have such fast and powerful machines all on the track together."[60] Instead each car had the track to itself for two warm-up laps and one speed lap. During the preliminaries the Stanley and Grout racers received the most attention, but the latter was withdrawn from the event because of a broken connecting rod. A special steam racer driven by Harvard student George Cannon also had the crowd's eye, and that afternoon it surpassed the Providence track record of the previous year in one minute and four and two-fifths seconds.[61]

It was the Stanley, shaped "like a cigar, painted red and called the Wogglebug," that set a new world's record for steamers in one minute and two and four fifths seconds.[62] A three-mile race for stock steamers, pitting Webb Jay's White against two Stanleys and a Locomobile, was won by a Stanley in four minutes and twenty-two seconds.[63]

Present that day were automobile experts from all over the nation and their attention was focused on the design and power plants of the racers. The *Automobile* magazine reported that F.E. Stanley's machine was

> the most radical departure from machines which he has operated before, but this was more in the boat-shaped body than in the mechanism. The operator's box gave access to the control levers in front, while a movable plate in the rear of the body gave an opportunity to get at the engine and pumps. The rig had a wheelbase of about eight feet and the wheels were fitted with wire spokes.[64]

Despite the attention given to steamers, the record set by the Stanley fell that very day. At the Empire City track near Yonkers, New York Barney Oldfield drove an eighty horsepower Ford racer a mile in one minute and three-fifths seconds.[65]

Encouraged by their racing triumphs the Stanley twins devoted more time to building racers. Two years after Readeville, they unveiled a 100-inch wheelbase machine equipped with a 205-pound engine which had a bore and stroke of $4\frac{1}{2}$ x $6\frac{1}{2}$ and a horsepower rating of 250. The boiler, 30 inches in diameter and 18 inches deep, could generate 1,000 pounds pressure. Fuel feed was controlled by two pressure tanks rated at 180 pounds per square inch.[66]

Dubbed the "Wogglebug" by the press, the racer was entered in the 1906 international speed trials held at Ormond Beach, Florida. This event, which attracted the fastest and most powerful cars in the world, was closely watched by the press and motoring public. In the fourth competition racing history was made by the Stanley steamer. Driven by Fred Marriot, head of the Stanley repair department, the "Wogglebug" set a new world's record of a mile in twenty-eight and one-fifth seconds. This is equivalent to a speed of 127.6 miles per hour and was only 2¾ miles "less than the fastest speed ever made on rails."[67] In its time this was exceptionally fast; the Stanley achievement was to stand for four years until Barney Oldfield, driving a Benz, beat it with a speed of 131.7 miles per hour.[68]

The Stanley twins were now determined to break their own record. During the fall and winter of 1906, many improvements were made on the "Wogglebug," including the addition of a larger boiler.[69] Also, two special Stanleys were built to compete in the Vanderbilt Cup Race, an event sponsored by the millionaire for whom the contest was named. Nevertheless, when these racers arrived at Ormond Beach, they were not permitted on the track because officials feared the exhaust steam would endanger the lives of the other contestants.[70] The "Wogglebug," however, was allowed to run in the international speed trials scheduled for January 25. Among the few cars registered for the contest was the first Rolls Royce to participate in a speed event in the United States.[71]

The spectators and reporters had anticipated something spectacular that day and they were not to be disappointed. With Marriot at the tiller, the "Wogglebug" hit the starting line under full throttle and sped along the sandy beach at top speed. What happened next is best described by Ray Stanley:

> When Marriot hit those little ripples on the sand they gave the front wheels a slight upward toss. The tremendous power at the rear wheels plus the lift from the car's springs raised the lighter front end of the car off the ground. Then the pressure of the air on the flat underside of the body acted like the force of air on the wing of an airplane, causing it to glide along with only the rear wheels on the ground. The car veered slightly to the left, toward the sea, and when the front wheels again touched, the racer rolled over and over and was dashed to pieces. The fact that Marriot escaped instant death was miraculous.[72]

According to F.E. Stanley the vehicle hit 150 m.p.h. at the time of the accident, but others claim a much higher speed.[73] Legend has it that the racer went 197 m.p.h. and took off like a rocket ship. In any event the evidence suggests that the "Wogglebug" could have reached 200 m.p.h. had the accident not occurred. No internal combustion propelled car could ever approach such a speed and few tried.

No one could deny that the steam car was the master of the racing world. Even the Lane brothers, whose sales amounted to no more than twelve vehicles a year, could boast of four victories by 1902.[74] In fact it was not until the Washington Park race held in June, 1900, that a gas car was able to prevail over a steamer.[75]

Up to this time the best of the American gas cars included the 26 h.p. Packard "Grey Wolf," the 80 h.p. Winton Bullet II, the 26 h.p. Ford "999," and the 20 h.p. Olds "Pirate." The Winton was particularly interesting. It had an eight-cylinder engine hung beneath a high chassis which was suspended on four wooden wheels. "It was cooled by a radiator that protruded in front like a bale of hay and the working parts were covered by a box-like enclosure."[76] In spite of its crude appearance it had won many races, including one over William K. Vanderbilt's 80 h.p. Mercedes in 1904.[77] In January of the same year the Packard "Grey Wolf" set three world's records in the Voiture Legere (light car) class at Daytona Beach. Only one American car, the 80 h.p. Winton Bullet II was faster, and that ran in the event for cars of any weight and horsepower.[78] Ford's "999" once set the record for the mile with a speed of 91.4 m.p.h. and continued to pile up victories in the ensuing years.[79]

Yet the very best gas racers could not equal the records set by steamers. Even the expensive foreign cars proved inadequate to this task. The reason for the gas car's comparatively poor showing is best stated by one expert:

> . . . the gasoline engine will never be the equal in performance of the steam engine until it is provided with a gear box having an infinite number of speeds; until the gears in the box change themselves without attention on the part of the driver. . . . and in such a way as to the ration best suited to the work at hand;

until the changes of gear are made without noise and without interruption of the tractive effort; until the engine secures overload capacity and starting torque, until it has some reserve of power, in some degree at least resembling the tremendous storage of energy provided by the hot water in the steam car's boiler . . .[80]

In fact the typical two-cylinder, double-acting steam engine had as many power impulses as an eight-cylinder gasoline engine; it also had a greater uniform torque delivered to its rear wheels "through the continued and overlapping admission of high-cylinder pressures."[81] The gas car had an advantage only in a long-distance event where the non-condensing steamer had to stop frequently for water. Thus the steamer was more than a match for its gasoline competition because its unique system of propulsion was ideally suited for automobile work.

VI

The Last of the Many

By 1910 the internal combusion engine was clearly the choice of most manufacturers. Only the Stanley twins still built steam cars and they carried on, despite dwindling sales, until 1924.[1] To all appearances the American steam car was dead; yet in 1916 a 21-year old genius named Abner Doble attempted a revival and almost succeeded.

Abner was born in 1895 into a prominent San Francisco family known for its engineering ability. His grandfather made miners' tools and his father produced a water wheel of his own design. Exposing his sons to mechanical matters at an early age, W.A. Doble had Abner and his three younger brothers, William, John and Warren, serve apprenticeships in the family factory.[2] In 1910 Abner enrolled at the Massachusetts Institute of Technology to study engineering but left in two years, after building several steam cars which he designated as Model A's. Improvements on these vehicles prompted him to form the Abner Doble Motor Vehicle Company of Waltham, Massachusetts.[3]

The performance of Abner's new roadster attracted so much attention that the Chalmers Motor Company hired the young inventor.[4] But he had ideas of his own and soon left the Chalmers Company to re-design his steamer, building the Models B and C, which had a two-cylinder, simple-expansion type engine and efficient condensers.[5] The latter gave the vehicles a range of 300 miles without a refill.[6] Even more remarkable was the fact that Doble's car could get between 13 and 15 miles to one gallon of kerosene and 10,000 miles on one gallon of oil.[7] Such a car did not escape the notice of the automobile world. The *Horseless Age* stated:

> The fuel is burned by means of a system that eliminates any attention or labor on the part of the driver, and reduces the time necessary to start the car from cold by the amount formerly necessary to properly pre-heat the vaporizer. This has been accomplished by taking a few pointers from the internal combustion engine design, in that air is made to pass through a device which mixes into it a correct amount of fuel and then this mixture is led into the combustion chamber where it is ignited by means of electricity. In order to cause the air to flow, a small blower, driven by an electric motor is used. This blower forces air through the carburetor into the combustion chamber and all that is necessary to start and run the car is to turn the switch to the running position, open the trottle and the car starts off.[8]

Such engineering advances were favorably received; it seemed that the starting problems associated with steamers of the past were solved. In fact the new boiler was capable of generating a full head of steam in less than three minutes. Of the water-tube type, its tubes were made from seamless drawn steel, ½ inch in diameter, welded into vertical grids. Operating pressure was 600 pounds, held constant by an automatic valve which controlled the fuel supply. There was little danger of an explosion as the boiler could withstand 8,000 pounds pressure and came equipped with a safety valve.[9]

In 1915 Doble joined with Claude P. Lewis, formerly head of the Consolidated Car Company, to form the General Engineering Corporation of Detroit, capitalized at $200,000.[10] Within two years the first production models were exhibited at the New

York Automobile Show and were considered by many to be the biggest hit since the event began. To insure the car's success some $10,000 worth of advertising was taken in national magazines at the time of its showing. This, it was claimed, brought in over 45,000 inquiries from buyers and dealers.[11] The company was quick to claim that "probably never before in the history of the automobile business has there been such a demand from high class dealers for territory as has developed since the introduction of the Doble-Detroit Steam car."[12] This was followed by a company boast that it had received orders for 11,000 cars in a ninety-day period.

Doble and his publicists appeared to be successful in bringing about a steam car revival and talked boldly of challenging the giants of the auto industry. Just as the factory geared up for production, however, the National War Emergency Board announced that no steel would be available for the duration of the war. General Engineering stopped production immediately and the hapless Doble was forced into creating another company.[13]

Before the war ended the Doble-Detroit Company became the successor firm with a capital of $1,000,000.[14] The Detroit *News* commented on the new company: "More than 1,100 dealers are already included in the Doble dealer organization and these have contracted for $12,000,000 worth of cars."[15] The vehicle, a vastly improved Model C, weighed 3,100 pounds and came with a 128-inch wheelbase. According to the company it had an advanced electric starting system and was more economical than the gas car.[16] A $3,750 three-passenger roadster and a $5,000 seven-passenger touring car were the only models made and were Doble's hope of cracking the high-priced car market.

In spite of much fanfare and stockholder confidence very few cars were actually built. Eventually wartime production problems and trouble with the advanced components caused the collapse of the company.[17] Particularly disappointing was the new uniflow expansion engine, which proved undesirable for high speeds because of its long heavy pistons.[18]

In 1919 Doble left the company and with the help of his brothers formed the Doble Steam Motors of California.[19] This time Abner was determined to succeed and purchased a small factory in San Francisco where he would make the Model D. He spent $100,000 on research alone, not only to produce a car free from defects but to prove steam superior to the internal combustion engine. In describing the new Doble car R. A. Wilson, representing the Commissioner of Corporations of the State of California, said:

> I put this boiler through some very severe tests and in no case did it fall down. I had a boiler taken out of a car after about 30,000 miles on the road and selected several sections of the boiler which were cut out and split open for inspection, and in all cases there was very little sediment and no scale. Next the water was all drained out of one of the boilers, and then the fire turned on the empty boiler. When the tubes reached the required heat, the fire automatically shut off, demonstrating that there was no danger of burning up a boiler. The water was fed into the boiler by four pumps, which are cut in and out by a very efficient selenoid device. In extremely heavy pulls, where the engine pumps are turning and giving a small water supply, there is an electric motor generator, which is driven from the water pump shaft.[20]

Each car came equipped with a four-cylinder, double-acting compound engine with two high pressure pistons operating the outside cranks and two low pressure pistons operating the two center cranks.[21] Steam to the engine was controlled by two piston valves of exclusive Doble design; each valve functioning for one high and one low pressure cylinder. With the engine integrated with the rear axle there was no need for a transmission, clutch or universal joints. J. N. Walton observed:

> . . . at sixty miles an hour this engine is turning over 900 revolutions per minute, as compared with a gas combustion engine turning over from 3,000 to 3,300 revolutions per minute. At 35 miles an hour the engine is turning over only 525 revolutions a minute, eliminating all vibration, friction and bearing pound.[22]

Of particular interest was the standard radiator serving as a condenser which was cooled by flowing air and a 24-inch fan. According to Doble the fan turned at 3,200 r.p.m. and could effectively handle exhaust steam at sixty miles per hour.[23]

The inventor was probably exaggerating on this point since at this rate of speed a much larger condenser would be needed to do the job properly. In any event the average cruising speed during the 1920's was 30 m.p.h. and at this rate the condenser certainly would be efficient. In fact the car was capable of traveling farther on 17 gallons of water at 30 m.p.h. than an internal combustion-propelled vehicle could go with 26 gallons of gasoline.

Doble further simplied the steam car by incorporating in its design a unit holding all the auxiliary apparatus. Included in it were the oil, water and vacuum pumps and the speedometer drive.[24] The water pumps were crank-driven and of the plunger type. Under normal conditions only two of these pumps were used, the remaining two cut in only when there was a heavy demand for steam.

Impressed with the new car, the Commissioner of Corporations permitted the Dobles to expand their operation. A prospectus was issued which stated: "The Doble Steam Motors is a Delaware Corporation with no preferred stock, having 500,000 shares of class A common stock at a par of 10 dollars a share and 5,000 shares of class B common."[26] The Doble brothers kept the B stock for themselves but would get no benefits until the class A stockholders received an eight per cent dividend.[27]

After more than ten years Abner Doble's efforts had paid off; the Model D was considered the best performing car in the country. The inventor would often prove this by putting his car through tests other motorists would never attempt. His favorite exhibition was to take the steamer to a steep grade and stop and start with ease at any point on the incline. It was also possible for him to drive "at 30 m.p.h., shift into reverse, slow to a smooth stop" and back up with great speed.[28] In February, 1924 the Automobile Club of America ran several tests to validate Doble's claims. The results left no doubt as to the car's superiority. After a night in an unheated garage it was reported that:

> In 23.1 seconds a stock Doble Phaeton generated a full head of steam from a dead cold with the thermostat set at 32 degrees F. . . . In 12.5 seconds the Doble, from a standstill, attained a

speed of 40 miles per hour. Later on the Doble car . . . accelerated from a standstill to 25 miles per hour in 5 seconds. In unofficial tests a Doble car accelerated from a standstill to 40 miles per hour in 8 seconds.[29]

Dobles could hit 95 miles per hour with ease and outrun any stock gas car built in the country. Of course a car with this performance was expensive. Prices for Dobles ranged from $8,000 for the runabout to $11,200 for the seven-passenger limousine. The latter proved to be popular although it weighed more than 4,200 pounds.[30] Discriminating customers also had the option of ordering custom built bodies from Murphy of California. Despite its price the car was a bargain when compared to its gasoline rivals. A typical Pierce Arrow with a six-cylinder engine sold for $5,250, the Franklin 6 for $1,950, the Lincoln V-8 for $3,800; and the Locomobile Touring Limousine was priced at $9,000.[31]

Only the very wealthy could afford Dobles and they bought the car sight unseen. Among the first to place orders were the celebrated Hollywood actress Norma Talmadge and the famous movie director Joseph Schenck. Howard Hughes and other millionaire bankers and industrialists also took delivery on the car. Purchasers from abroad included the Maharajah of Bharatpur and prominent figures in England, Germany and New Zealand.[32]

With renewed interest in steam power Doble believed there was room for a steamer in the popular priced car market. The new car, which would sell for $2,000, was designed around the Jordan "big 6" chassis and came equipped with V-shaped 4 cylinder uniflow expansion engine of forty horsepower.[33] Preliminary testing, however, proved the engine to be inefficient; more research was necessary before the car was ready for manufacture. By April, 1924 Doble's new factory at Emeryville, California was capable of turning out 300 Model E's a year and a projected addition to this plant would raise production to 1,000 cars.[34]

Just as Doble was in a position to challenge the gas car disaster struck. Throughout 1923 and 1924 stock traders illegally manipulated Doble stock, ruining the company's reputation. Doble's attempt to release the promised stock failed and several lawsuits followed. In a criminal action he was held "technically liable" and sentenced to prison; fortunately the sentence was reversed by a higher court.[35]

For all practical purposes the company was ruined but Doble continued his research, eventually producing a small number of Model F steamers, the last cars he made. The 1929 stock market crash, though, put an end to Doble's American operations and in 1931 the company went into liquidation.[36]

The steam car revival, however, was not limited to one car. During the post war years at least eleven other companies brought out cars, trucks or buses:

Vehicle	Location	Dates
American	Chicago, Illinois	1922-1924
Baker	Denver, Colorado; Cleveland, Ohio	1921-1927
Brooks	Stratford, Ontario	1923-1926
Bryan	Peru, Indiana	1918-1923
Coats	Columbus, Ohio; Chicago, Illinois	1921-1924
Curran-Nebelmesser	New York City	1928
Delling	Camden, New Jersey	1923-1927
Gearless	Pittsburgh, Pennsylvania	1921-1924
MacDonald	Garfield, Ohio	1923
Scott-Newcomb	St. Louis, Missouri	1920-1923
Trask-Detroit	Detroit, Michigan	1922

Each of them entered the market with a flourish of hope and optimism and each ended in a resounding failure. With the exception of the Brooks they produced no more than a few prototypes. Speaking of the Scott-Newcomb car produced by the Standard Engineering Company of St. Louis, Missouri, the *Scientific American* stated that "we find ingenious people continuously putting forward new versions of the ultimate car propelled by steam."[37] This comment could also be applied to any of the others. When the Delling steam car was introduced by automobile designer Eric H. Delling of West Collingwood, New Jersey it was said that:

. . . it is by no means a stretch of the imagination to predict that Camden will be the home of the world's most famous steam-propelled automobile. The Delling Steam Car—the only car that meets every demand—is a Camden built product. . . . It won't be long before Delling steam cars are a common sight on Camden's highways.[38]

The Brooks Steam Motors of Stratford, Ontario, Canada had much better success than the others even though they made no more than 300 cars. Selling for $3,885.00 the five passenger sedan was different from other cars because of the Meritas waterproof fabric which covered its entire body, one good reason for the Brooks' early success. The company said that:

> the most advanced type of body construction has been adopted by several of the largest British manufacturers and is rapidly gaining popularity in this country. The advantages of the fabric over wood, steel or aluminum are numerous. The driver of the Brooks sedan will immediately note the absence of rumbling and vibrations. Body squeaks and rattles are eliminated.[39]

At the height of the steam car revival George A. Coats of Sandusky, Ohio offered the public a $1,000 steam car.[40] Much advertising space was taken in trade journals and the widely distributed brochure included this rhyme:

> George is the bird
>   Of whom you've heard,
> His friends called him a dreamer;
>   But, your life you may stake
> He is wide awake
>   On how to build a steamer.[41]

Men like Duncan MacDonald, it appeared, never gave up. His name crops up in 1923 in connection with the Gearless Motor Corporation swindle in which $1,114,000 worth of securities were falsely sold.[42] That same year he promoted another car called the "Bobcat" which he built in Garfield, Ohio.[43] In 1930 he joined with Jeffery Carqueville in converting a Nash touring car to steam.[44]

Mechanically the new steamers incorporated many

advances. The Gearless had a burner which could be easily disassembled for cleaning every 5,000 miles; its two two-cylinder double-acting engines were connected directly to the rear axle and eliminated the need for a differential.[45] The Standard could run a mile "on stored steam after the fire is shut off."[46] Dr. Hartley O. Baker, the Denver surgeon, said that "no other known boiler can be as thoroughly, quickly and easily cleaned with its own pressure as the Baker boiler."[47] Eric H. Delling claimed his car had a 62 horsepower engine which turned only 1,200 r.p.m. at 60 m.p.h.[48]

A last attempt to break the monopoly of the gas car was attempted by Frank Curran and Charles Nebelmesser. In 1928 these young inventors developed a steam bus which prompted the *Scientific American* to state that "it has been so successful that the old questions of the relative value of steam and gasoline propulsion have been revived with considerable pertinency."[49]

The Curran steam bus was powered by a three-cylinder reciprocating uniflow engine of 185 horsepower which, engineers claimed, "developed one horsepower for every 22 pounds of steam consumed."[50] A seamless boiler, encased entirely in aluminum, generated steam at 600 pounds pressure. The vaporizing type burner could burn gasoline or kerosene efficiently.[51]

A superior performer to the gasoline bus, it was the perfect answer to the problem of noise and air pollution which plagued metropolitan traffic at the time. The *Scientific American* said:

> To the average person who must frequent streets which are crowded with traffic, the elimination, at least in part, of some of the obnoxious gases which are the products of combustion in the gasoline engine, will be welcomed as a wholesome boon, for clean air to breathe is rapidly becoming at a premium and no one realizes it more than he who must inhale, almost without hesitation the atmosphere which is now part of his daily routine.[52]

The editor of *Automotive Industries* foresaw the future:

> It will not do for the manufacturers to permanently ignore this situation. Unless they cooperate toward the abatement of the present nuisance and possible menace to health, stringent regulations

ultimately will compel them to bring about improved conditions, in the meantime hampering the sale of their product.[53]

The automobile industry rejected the Curran steam bus and this signalled the end of the steam car revival. Despite its many drawbacks the internal combustion engine was now clearly the master of mechanical transportation.

Although the steam car of the twenties was a vast improvement over its predecessors, offering economy, speed and power, the giants of the automobile industry—Ford, General Motors, Studebaker, Chrysler, Packard and Willys—would have no part of it. Selling the already established gasoline cars was profitable and the public was satisfied with them. Henry Ford had put the nation on wheels with his Model T, which sold for as little as $260 in 1925.[54] In fact, by 1920, half the cars in the country were "tin lizzies" and this situation was due to Ford's assembly-line techniques. Why change? And what manufacturer of steamers could compete with the mass-produced car?

Of course the public got just what it paid for. The Model T was underpowered, noisy, hard-riding and in general a poor performer. Equipped with a four-cylinder twenty-horsepower engine, its speed was limited to 42 m.p.h. and every hill drained its energy. The only positive features of the car were its simplicity and economy. Fuel consumption was between 25 to 30 miles to the gallon.[55]

Starting and driving the T required considerable attention and effort. Although the self-starter had been available since 1912 it was not a popular option because of the added cost. To start the car drivers first set the spark advance, situated on the hub of the steering wheel, so as to retard the spark. They then proceeded to the front of the vehicle and with one hand pulled the choke wire, using the other hand to crank the starter.[56] If the spark advance was left in an advanced setting or if the various starting components were out of adjustment, the crank handle would kick back and could cause serious injury to the driver. Cranking the gas car was not a job for the ladies.

Once the car was started the driver manipulated three foot

pedals, two of which engaged the planetary type transmission, giving the vehicle two forward speeds and one speed in reverse. The third pedal operated the brake. When the extreme left-hand pedal was depressed and held, the transmission was engaged in low gear; a quick release of the pedal engaged the driving or high gear. Equipped with a commutator, which regulated the current to the spark plug, and a timer which opened and closed the contact bringing about a single spark, the Model T's ignition system was complex to say the least. Its single throat carburetor also required periodic cleaning and adjustment to prevent stalling. The engine had a life-span of from 10,000 to 15,000 miles before a carbon and valve job was needed, an expensive chore for drivers of limited means.[57]

The typical steamer of the twenties had no clutch, no carburetor, no drive shaft, no commutator or distributor and no transmission. It could cruise at 65 m.p.h. with ease and reach speeds of 90 m.p.h. without the slightest difficulty. Starting required only the turn of an ignition switch and a wait of approximately a minute. Steam generating plants were safe, non-stallable, silent and did not pollute the air. With their few components there was less chance of a breakdown. The Doble engine had only 35 moving parts, the Brooks 38. Typical Dobles traveled more than 200,000 miles without an engine overhaul and it was reported that a Doble E-14 went 600,000 miles without any trouble whatsoever.[58]

The steamer used kerosene, selling for 9 cents a gallon, which was consumed at the same rate as by the gas car at speeds under 40 m.p.h. The Model T used gasoline, which cost between 23 and 25 cents a gallon. In short, the gasoline car, whether it was a Model T or a luxurious Packard, came off second best in comparison to the steamer. Why then did the steam car revival of the twenties fail? The answer can be found in the attitude of the major automobile manufacturers who found no need to adopt another power while business was good. The public was buying the gasoline car and presumably liked it the way it was, therefore there was no need to change. The builder of steamers, without the funds to compete with the giants, could only hope that one of the large firms would become interested in his products.

One may speculate on the possibility of the Ford Motor Company, for example, mass producing a steamer. The price of such a car would have been competitive, but of course Ford would have had to shut down its factories producing clutches, carburetors, drive-shafts and transmissions. Since the steam engine was long-wearing, the need for replacement parts would have been curtailed. In fact the independent supplier of spark plugs, commutators, valve springs and crank handles would have been put out of business altogether. Such a situation would certainly have caused a revolution in the auto industry and profoundly affected the nation's economy. The major oil companies would have been affected by the introduction of a mass-produced steamer, at least during the 1920's. By 1919 85 per cent of the total domestic distribution of 87.5 million barrels of gasoline was purchased by owners of gas cars.[59] The consumption of such a volume indicated that selling gasoline was profitable and the more gas cars the bigger the profits. Kerosene, on the other hand, was a cheap by-product of petroleum cracking which was less volatile and not as explosive as gasoline. If the demand for kerosene exceeded that of gasoline the oil companies, with their huge investments in refineries and complicated equipment, would have suffered.

The steam car would have to wait for more favorable conditions to make a comeback.

VII

The Battle Is Over

In determining the reasons for the failure of the steam car one must look to consumer preference, for as early as 1901 the public had decided on the gas car. The question why they picked the inferior motive power certainly needs to be answered. Price was not a factor in their choice as the first steamers were competitive in this respect. In fact the Wood listed for $450 and the Mobile runabout was $550, considerably cheaper than the popular curved dash Olds, which sold for $650.

Riding quality and silent operation must also be discounted as factors since steamers excelled in these categories. The available evidence indicates that many hospitals preferred the White ambulance for just these reasons. Steamers also excelled in power, speed and performance as shown by their long list of victories in hillclimbs, endurance runs and circuit racing. In 1906, the Stanley racer achieved a speed of 127.6 m.p.h., establishing a record which stood for four years until Barney Oldfield beat it by less than three miles per hour.

No one could deny that steam was the most powerful motive power one could buy. One prominent engineer, in a letter to the *Scientific American,* said that:

> Of course at 10 miles per hour the engine cannot develop 70 horsepower, but it can develop more than three times as much power as an eight cylinder gasoline engine can develop at that speed. At 20 miles per hour the steamer can develop between two and three times as much power as the gas car, and at 30 m.p.h. the available power of the steamer is about double that of the gas car.[1]

With the steam the driver was getting more than he needed and with an engine speed a third of the gas car. Every automobile designer knew that

> it is the pull or push of the tire on the road that is effective in the propulsion of a car. Witness the utter absurdity of a steam car equipped with a 20 horsepower engine outpacing and outclimbing gas cars the engines of which will develop up to 80 horsepower on the block. The steam car does this by greater and more uniform torque delivered to its rear wheels.[2]

What may have prompted buyers to purchase the gas car was the thought that steamers were too complex. Steamers certainly had their share of valves and regulating wheels which required frequent manipulation. To start the very early steamers the driver had to perform several procedures which included checking the steam, water, fuel and air systems. On most steamers the fuel and air pressure had to be raised by hand pumping. An acetylene torch was usually applied to ignite the fuel in the pilot. Operating pressure was raised in seven to fifteeen minutes if a White and fifteen to thirty minutes if a Stanley, but what is frequently overlooked is that 200 pounds pressure could be maintained in idle steamers by leaving the pilot burning. Thus after a night in a garage, the steamer was ready to go instantly. The advances made in steam cars of the twenties reduced starting time to approximately one minute. Unfortunately such technological progress came too late.

Prior to 1912, all manufacturers of gas cars provided the owner with a booklet giving detailed information on starting and operating procedures. A quick glance at this literature proves that a driver could not operate this type car unless he was completely informed about many technical details. Starting alone was a difficult chore. After setting the spark advance, choking and cranking, the Reo company advised that:

> It is well worth the time spent in practice to be able to use exactly the right spark under all conditions. . . . You will note that the throttle is controlled by hand and foot levers which operate independently of each other. It is perhaps best for inexperienced drivers to attempt the use of the foot lever only.[3]

The 1909 Maxwell booklet listed fifteen different instructions which a driver had to follow before he could get underway.[4] The company undoubtedly presumed that purchasers of its cars had intelligence, patience, skill and a strong arm.

No steamer handbook could match the directions printed in the 1909 Packard booklet. Almost a miniature textbook, its 56 pages not only discussed starting and operating procedures but also described the vehicle's components. Directions for starting took five pages, indicating that this was not a chore for a novice. The company made it clear that

> the beginner crank the motor with the switch off because then there is absolutely no danger. . . . We would suggest that, in cranking with the switch on, the left hand be used engaging the crank near its lowest point. . . . and lifting quickly over compression. Cranking the motor in this manner with the left hand, if by oversight the spark be advanced, the kick of the motor would merely pull the handle out of your fingers; whereas should you push down on the handle a serious sprain might result to your wrist or hand.[5]

The company might also have added that one could be thrown to the ground with a broken arm.

In 1912, Charles Kettering, an electrical engineer employed by Dayton Engineering Laboratories Company (DELCO) solved this problem by perfecting a self-starter for Cadillac.[6] Vincent Bendix, the innovative inventor, added the starter drive, thus making the electric starter a prominent feature of the gas car. This device, however, did not force the steamer from the market.

Sales of gas cars had already surpassed steam cars by 1902, and in 1912 only Stanley remained. Thus the self-starter can be eliminated as a reason for the decline of the steam car.

Although both cars were complex, it was the steamer that required more attention to operate. Early drivers had to watch a waterglass which showed the water level in the boiler. On most Stanleys the glass was situated on the dash and lighted by a carbide lamp for night driving. On the Grout it was placed on the right side of the body, near the front fender, (Grouts had right-hand drive) so as not to distract the driver's attention from the road. The fuel, steam, air and water gauges also required periodic glances. Faced with a water-glass and several gauges many buyers believed the vehicle required more attention than it actually did, and in consequence bought gas cars. This, however, was not a major reason for the steamer's decline.

The myth that steamers were useless in winter must also be ignored as a reason for the car's unpopularity. Actually steamers were better suited for winter use than gas cars because of their stored heat. Stanleys could be left in unheated garages overnight, in zero weather, and be ready to go in minutes. As long as the pilot light was burning 200 pounds pressure could be maintained and the flame could burn unattended for several days.[7] The company even claimed that its cars could be left out in zero weather with undrained water tanks. "They have frozen and thawed a dozen times, beyond bursting a pipe or two—nothing critical or expensive," was the boast of an early brochure.[8]

By comparison gas cars required constant attention in cold weather. In the days before anti-freeze drivers added boiling water to radiators before starting. Solutions containing calcium chloride or a mixture of glycerine and water were both used, but both concoctions were ineffective and frequently damaged hoses. To avoid a cracked motor block the wise driver usually garaged his car for the entire winter.

The driver of the gas car that did venture out in the winter usually got bogged down in heavy snow. On the other hand it was rare to see the steamer rendered helpless in snow or mud since the driver had stored power at his disposal. The reserve power in the boiler and the engine's ability to utilize excessive steam allowed these vehicles to achieve tremendous momentary traction. This is probably one good reason why the President and the United States Army found the steam car suitable for all types of driving conditions. Steam was reliable and one expert explained that

> a gasoline engine requires the exact fulfillment of several easily realized conditions in order that it shall operate. Unless they are properly realized the engine may not run at all. If they are fulfilled the engine is perfectly automatic and capable of doing its work indefinitely.
>
> The steam engine is somewhat different in this respect. It is not quite so particular as to the conditions. It may be badly out of adjustment and repair, but when the steam reaches it something generally has to turn around. It may operate very badly indeed, but it will keep on moving when conditions are most unfavorable, because it has the boiler . . . and although it may leak steam at every point, it will most likely not entirely refuse to "mote" as long as nothing breaks.[9]

Poor fuel economy was another charge leveled against steamers. Before 1906, steamers consumed gasoline at the rate of seven miles per gallon, except for the White which got close to thirteen miles per gallon. Such a high rate of consumption was due to the combustion that took place outside of the cylinder, causing the heat of combustion to be transferred by conduction through the walls of the boiler to the water that did the work. During this process much heat was wasted. The best thermal efficiency of a steam generating plant was between sixteen and twenty per cent.[10] In 1906, it was claimed that the best internal combustion motors "have converted thirty-five per cent of the heat of combustion into work, or twice as much as the best steam engines."[11] Of course with improved generators and burners, and with the switch to a cheap fuel such as kerosene, steam cars became more economical. A 4,550 pound Doble E-19 could obtain about fourteen miles to the gallon of kerosene which cost approximately nine cents a gallon.[12] Thus it cost only eighteen cents to travel 28 miles. A gas car of equivalent size could get only eighteen miles to a gallon of gasoline, which cost 23 cents a gallon, proving that the steamer was cheaper to operate. It was even more economical than the 1,200 pound Model T which cost its operator 23 cents to travel 25 miles.

The huge consumption of water appears to be the most uneconomical feature of steamers. Even during the 1920's steam cars were still unable to effectively condense steam at speeds over thirty miles an hour. According to steam engineer William Besler:

> The condenser is the death knell of the possibility of a steam vehicle, as people visualize it, as something with unlimited power. The more power, logically the larger the condenser. With even medium-sized engines, the condenser has to be huge, providing at least ten square feet of frontal area per 100 continuous horse-power.[13]

Besler's statement is true, but not applicable to steamers of the past because the average speed of those vehicles was under forty miles per hour. Poor roads, inadequate suspensions and easily punctured tires were the real factors that limited a car's speed. The condensers were therefore adequate for the stresses placed on them.

The steam car's image was probably the most important factor in discouraging prospective buyers. Equipped with a burner that generated a roaring flame under a wooden chassis, and a boiler that had the potential of exploding, the steamer was considered by many to be a dangerous contraption. Although this writer has evidence that no more than two boiler explosions occured among the thousands of steamers produced, the belief that steamers were unsafe was widespread. It grew up from the hundreds of fires and explosions resulting from defective or improperly cared for marine and stationary steam engines. It was this factor, more than anything else, that caused an aura of distrust to surround the steam engine.

With such events fresh in his mind the average purchaser of automobiles was naturally reluctant to sit over or behind a roaring fire in a steam car. Many a sale was lost when the fire flared up scorching the wooden frame and singeing the driver's trousers. By 1905, a number of major insurance companies had already excluded certain steam cars from coverage. A few years earlier New York's boiler inspectors demanded that steam car drivers be licensed. The roaring fire and boiler-under-the-seat design certainly inhibited the success of early Locomobiles, Stanleys and Mobiles. The gasoline car, despite its drawbacks, offered the buyer peace of mind and it therefore became the choice of the majority.

It was amazing that sales of steamers even kept pace with the gas car in view of public fears and hostile bankers. Of the more than 137 firms that produced this type car, only a few survived more than two years. Many of them began by issuing large amounts of securities based more on hope than anything else and only the public's faith in the steam car's speed and reliability kept the larger companies in business. Without a merger, builders of steamers competed against each other and against their powerful rivals who made gas cars. Foster, Stearns, Century and Rochester, with factories in upstate New York, soon collapsed after their local markets were exhausted. To survive these firms needed sales more than anything else. With hostile bankers and an unstable market, only an increased output could save them. According to Lawrence Seltzer:

> Increases in their output, stimulated both by the rapidly growing general demand and by the cumulative growth in the reputations of particular makes, did not require immediate and large additions to their plants nor to their working capital. The facilities of partsmakers steadily increased; competition among distributors and dealers for the profitable sales rights permitted the continuance of the practice of advance dealer deposits and cash sales. . . . It was in this way that Buick, Ford, Cadillac, Maxwell and Olds and other producers grew.[14]

Advertising, of course, was the only medium which could convince the public that steam was safe. The theme, however, of most steam car advertisements was speed and power, and little was said about the disadvantages of the gasoline motor. Makers of gas cars, on the other hand, stressed luxury, quality and speed in their advertisements and were able to convince the public that their product was the equal of the steam car.

Trends were set very easily, as one pioneer advertising man stated:

> People follow styles and preferences. We rarely decide for ourselves, because we don't know the facts. But when we see the crowds taking any certain direction we are much inclined to go with them. [15]

The Stanley twins never advertised at all, while the remaining firms displayed little imagination in their promotion campaigns. Many companies, realizing the public's preference for the internal combustion engine, attempted to jump on the band wagon to save themselves. Grout and White did this and were therefore able to forestall bankruptcy.

The revival of the twenties brought with it many improvements in steam plant design. The atomizer, the electric ignition, the thermo-electric water gauge, the improved compound engine and the new flash boiler made the steamer the best performer on the road. It could start in less than a minute, accelerate to a hundred miles an hour in a few seconds, be reversed at thirty miles an hour and offered silent and smooth operation. More important, though, was that it did not pollute the air. At a time when the gas car dominated urban thoroughfares, toxic fumes in the air prompted comment by many automobile and health authorities. Albert Clough, staff writer for the *Horseless Age*, stated:

> The combustion of gasoline in an internal combustion motor produces a decidedly different and more objectionable odor, which is compounded of gasoline, imperfectly consumed and of volatized and imperfectly altered cylinder oil which escapes from the hot cylinder walls with the exhaust. The occupants of a motor vehicle are seldom troubled by this odor, but in the interest of the general public, it should be reduced to the lowest practicable point. [16]

In 1906, Professor Charles Dewar, a Cambridge University chemist, attracted much attention with his warning that the exhaust of gas cars was poisonous and rendered the air in city streets unfit to breathe. [17] A report was also circulated in the press at the time that Baroness Hengelmaller, wife of the Austrian ambassador at Washington, "was using a preparation for scenting the exhaust of her car, which left a trail of violet and other sweet fumes."[18]

Surely the treatment of exhaust fumes with perfume was a futile effort to hide the toxic fumes, but the builders of gas cars certainly had no better answer. The Curran steam bus, developed in 1928, could have alleviated this problem, but it was rejected at the time because the automobile industry was controlled by devotees of the internal combustion engine. Air pollution would therefore remain a major problem of the big cities. Without the funds to mass produce a steamer, every manufacturer failed, and the steam car revival of the twenties collapsed.

Perhaps the fate of the steamer would have been altered if there was more vigorous leadership. The genius of a Durant, an Olds or a Ford, with their talent for dealing with the mass mind and the mass market, was badly needed. Public fear and reluctance could then be overcome by an extensive advertising campaign, but once this was done steam would again become the motive power of the nation.

Steam Now

The cry "bring back the steam car" is now uttered with increasing frequency by those familiar with the nation's health, energy and transportation problems. The reasons are clear. Life in the cities is increasingly dangerous to our health. Los Angeles is enveloped by smog, caused primarily by gas cars, for more than eight months a year. New York City was found to have the highest concentration of carbon monoxide in the nation with as much as 5.29 million tons being emitted into the air annually.[1] Only a few years ago the carbon monoxide level in downtown Chicago measured 15 parts per million, nine parts beyond the safe level.[2]

Everyone knows that the nation's health is directly affected by the emissions of internal combustion engines. Many Americans were startled when the New York Tuberculosis and Health Association reported back in March, 1970 that there was a 500 per cent increase in emphysema and a 20 per cent increase in chronic bronchitis deaths in New York City alone.[3] The Sloan-Kettering Institute has stated:

> If you collect the solid material from automobile exhaust and purify it to the extent that you presumably isolate the een-compounds and do the same thing with cigarette smoke, you find that the purified compounds from exhaust smoke are twice as likely to cause skin cancer in mice as those from cigarettes.[4]

The situation became so serious that in 1970 Congress passed and the President signed Public Law 90-148, popularly known as the Clean Air Act. In compliance with its provisions the Environmental Protection Agency set rigid air standards to limit the amount of dangerous pollutants emitted into the air.[5]

American and foreign auto manufacturers were expected to substantially reduce the amounts of hydrocarbons, nitrogen oxides and particulates, with a "90 per cent reduction in carbon monoxide" alone.[6] Thereafter these poisons are to be present only in negligible amounts. Government figures showing permissible emissions in grams per mile for 1976 are:

Hydrocarbons   0.41
Carbon Monoxide   3.4
Oxides of Nitrogen 0.4[7]

Noise pollution is another danger associated with internal combustion engines. In January, 1972, New Jersey became the first state in the union to pass a noise abatement law, which now serves as a model for other states.[8] A month later the Environmental Protection Agency issued a 301-page report which "confirmed that noise is an insidious form of pollution that may affect at least 80 million Americans."[9] *Newsweek Magazine* reported that "E.P.A. researchers found that the roar of automobiles, buses and trucks at rush hour in New York City or Los Angeles frequently runs ninety decibels." A decibel is a measure of sound intensity and 100 decibels is considered deafening.[10] Snowmobiles, the latest product of internal combustion technology are rated at 108 decibels.[11] The gasoline engine is frequently regarded as the villain which has upset America's equilibrium.

Noise is also associated with speed and power, selling points to parts of America's youth market. All sorts of promotion addressed to the teenager tell him how he can alter his new car or jalopy to give the impression he is driving an Indianapolis 500 racer. He can do this by increasing its noise capability, i.e., adding a high compression manifold, dual exhausts and a special carburetor. The result is an ear-splitting, gas-gurgling behemoth. The Supreme Muffler Company advertised its "orange peeler" as being capable of "low back pressure, the peeler steps up engine performance, its deep throaty sound of power starts with two kinds of exclusive fiberglass packing."[12] The Arvin Muffler Company claims "it has a goodie for you that steps up your go power . . . with a turned on sound."[13]

For those unwilling to make these deafening modifications Chrysler Corporation offers its "hemi-cuda car, its angriest, slipperiest looking body shell, wrapped around ol' King Kong hisself."[14] Equipped with dual exhausts, special camshafts, a four-barrel carburetor and a four-speed Hurst transmission, it is Detroit's answer to noise abatement and control. General Motors, the industry's leader in innovation has its Chevelle SS 396 to match the hemi-cuda, while Ford's "better idea" is the Mercury Cougar XR-7 or Mustang Boss 302.

With these air- and noise-pollution dangers compounded by the fuel crises a new breed of realists is producing a competitive steam car. The contributions of William P. Lear to technology have been legion. Born in Hannibal, Missouri in 1903, he holds 130 patents and is credited with a number of pioneering inventions, among which are the first car radio, the first aircraft automatic pilot, the first eight-track stereo tape player and the first business jet aircraft.[15] At twenty-six he developed the Majestic radio and a few years later helped create Motorola Corporation.[16]

Lear Motors Corporation, his Nevada based firm, was founded in 1968, with the objective of producing "a real-world power system that not only equals today's conventional engines, but surpasses them in every way."[17] This "power system" is the turbine engine adapted to the Rankine cycle. In operation,

> Water is converted to steam in the vapor generator by a combustor fueled by kerosene or other low cost fuel. The steam is directed against the turbine blades through small nozzles causing the turbine to rotate. Turbine rotation is translated to the driveshaft through gear reduction and a conventional automatic transmission. Steam passing through a condenser is cooled to a liquid and retained for use again.[18]

The boiler or vapor generator is "about the size of a spare tire" and is exceptionally efficient. According to the company "heat transfer to the working fluid is so complete that a bare hand can be placed on the exterior housing of the boiler without harm."[19] When the generator output was 50 h.p. the boiler efficiency was 96 per cent; it was 89 per cent when at 250 h.p., the peak power output.[20] The California State Assembly was particularly pleased and in its *Steam Bus Newsletter* stated that the Lear system is "simple and because it embodies a turbine drive, it appears to be economical to manufacture and maintain."[21] The Lear bus can meet the 1976 Clean Air Act standards and this has buoyed hopes in California. In anticipation of the future Lear Motors has developed a small unit suitable for automobiles.[22]

Others have also been successful in producing new "steam systems." Wallace J. Minto has already earned much fame with his flourocarbon car. Born in 1922 in Jersey City, New Jersey, he displayed his genius at an early age.[23] One report claims that at ten Minto was reading advanced chemistry textbooks and by sixteen had discovered Plutonium, an element used in the manufacture of the atom bomb.[24]

As head of Kinetics Corporation of Sarasota, Florida he has developed a propulsion system which substitutes flourocarbon for water, thus eliminating the condensing problems common in steam cars of the past. In Minto's car the power system resembles a conventional steam plant in many respects, except that the old slide valve engine is done away with. The unit consists of a heat exchanger, a drive motor, a condensor and a pump.[25] The heat to operate the heat exchanger is provided by blower and pump fed burners which accept either kerosene or gasoline. According to Minto:

> In the heat exchanger, the heat from the burners is used to boil refrigerant liquid UCON-113 (Freon). The UCON-113 vapor passes from the heat exchanger to the drive motor through a throttle valve. The throttle valve (operated by the accelerator pedal) controls the pressure and amount of vapor entering the drive motor, and therefore the speed of the car. UCON-113 vapor from the heat exchanger also goes to a small auxiliary motor which runs the alternator. From these two motors the vapor passes into a condensor where it is changed back to a liquid.[26]

According to the company reports, the new engine's exhaust is "more than 200 times cleaner than will be required by the 1980 H.E.W. standards."[27] The Minto steamer is so quiet that one would hardly notice its presence. The engine need not be "revved up" when starting out in the morning or at red lights. In fact there is no muffler because the fuel "is burned nonexplosively."[28] Nissan Motors of Japan was quick to enter into an agreement with Kinetics Corporation and already has produced successful prototypes.[29]

The much publicized Williams brothers of Ambler, Pennsylvania have been working on a marketable steam car since 1940. In a family of five brothers, twins Calvin and Charles have been following the steam car tradition set by their engineer father Calvin C., who was awarded a number of patents on steam motor designs.[30] In 1966, the twins distributed a brochure describing their system; for $10,250 they could deliver a steam converted Chevrolet Chevelle.[31] Promising though it seemed, their project failed because, as Calvin stated before a Senate Committee:

> We just couldn't get any kind of deliveries on castings. Steel, bearings and the cost of things skyrocketed. For example we use these timing chain sprockets to drive the camshafts. We had purchased these sprockets in small quantities before. Come time to order them for these ten units, the price jumped from $24

a sprocket to $77 a sprocket. We thought that was quite a jump. It has been that way practically on every item we use.[32]

Unable to overcome such suspect stumbling blocks, the twins closed down their small factory, but in the fall of 1971 their luck changed. The First Pennsylvania Bank of Philadelphia granted them $500,000 for operating capital and a $350,000 mortgage.[33] The bank executive, George A. Butler, stated: "There is no question that this engine has great potential for automobiles and as a solution to the pollution problem."[34] Mr. Butler was referring to a unique 105-cubic-inch motor, a combination of the uniflow and counterflow types, which could burn diesel fuel or gasoline, "averaging close to twenty miles per gallon."[35] Capable of generating 650 pounds per square inch and 150 horsepower, it can propel the car at speeds exceeding 130 m.p.h. No gasoline automobile can match this performance with an engine of similar size.[36]

Many others have been reviving the steam car. In Melbourne, Australia Edward Pritchard has built a truck and car that hold much promise. In testimony given before the panel on Environmental Science and Technology in March, 1972, Captain Richard G. Alexander, representing the Pancoastal Corporation, which has studied the Pritchard car, stated:

> . . . . With regard to reliability, I can state that the Pritchard steam car operated satisfactorily through a series of tests involving about 125 miles of city driving, with some freeway driving, under a variety of conditions. The steam car's performance, in comparison with another vehicle identical to it except for its internal combustion engine, was equal to the comparison car in extended city driving tests.[37]

Throughout the entire test, the Pritchard steamer was operating at approximately "70 per cent of its designed power output."[38] The steam generating unit, installed in a 1963 Ford Falcon, consisted of a V-4 uniflow engine weighing about 125 pounds. The boiler is a monotube coil thirteen inches in diameter and 15½ inches high. A burner, located at the base of the boiler, is driven by a 12 volt electric motor, which also runs the fuel pump and air blower. A condenser, similar to an automobile radiator, has been found to be quite satisfactory under all conditions.[39] The Pritchard steamer with some improvements should be able to meet 1976 E.P.A. standards.[40]

Gene van Grecken, an enterprising Australian inventor and businessman, has built a $250,000 racer capable of developing 400 horsepower at 3,000 revolutions per minute. One writer has said that the Gvang steamer "is unlike any design previously produced, with two large pistons that oscillate but do not revolve completely. . . . this is the biggest single advantage of his design and makes possible an exceptionally high power to weight ratio."[41] The 163.5-inch-long, 65-inch-wide car is capable of 200 m.p.h. and will attempt to break the 1906 record of 127.6 m.p.h. held by the Stanley steamer.[42]

James L. Dooley of the McCulloch Corporation of Los Angeles, who acquired the patents on Abner Doble's steamers has been conducting research toward improving the famous car's engine and generator.[43] Reports of a steam car built in Crystal River, Florida have also attracted much attention. James Hyde of Hyde Power Systems Inc. has developed a steamer with a five-cylinder piston engine in each front wheel. All systems are completely automatic and require little attention from the driver.[44]

The Geni Power Company of Portland, Oregon has entered the market with its little steam-propelled sports vehicle. The company states: "we have successfully duplicated the early Stanley performance and reliability . . . while having done away with the complicated two fuel system, fire-prone burner."[45] Equal in size to a Volkswagen, the Geni can go from 0-60 m.p.h. in 16 seconds. It is ready to move in 95 seconds. Drivers are advised to use stove oil which the car guzzles at 12.5 m.p.g.[46]

Thus far the evidence indicates that a competitive and marketable steam car built with modern technology is on the way. Modern steam systems, like their predecessors, are superior to their internal combustion and diesel engine counterparts. A new steam bus demonstrated before government officials and several Congressmen, has already proved this point. Built by William M. Brobeck and Associates of Berkeley, California for the AC Transit Company, it carried its passengers in comfort and safety in demonstrations held in Washington, D.C. "Congressional reaction was enthusiastic," stated one report, because AC Transit Bus No. 666 outperformed Detroit's best diesel-powered bus of similar size."[47] Observers were particularly impressed by the big bus's quiet and smooth ride. With a gross vehicle weight of 30,580 pounds (equal to 51 passengers), the vehicle

> reached a top speed of 56 m.p.h. compared to an identical coach with a Detroit diesel 6V-71 engine and a 25,320 pound load equal to thirty passengers. Acceleration times in elapsed seconds were almost identical between coaches, even though the steam bus carried a heavier load. [48]

Of even greater importance is the bus's low-emission capabilities. Initial figures indicate that

> For carbon monoxide, the steam bus recorded 2.0 grams, the V-6 diesel 4.4 grams and the V-8 diesel 7.9 grams . . . With respect to nitrogen dioxide and hydrocarbons combined, the steam bus emitted 2.4 grams, the V-6 diesel 11.5 grams and the V-8 diesel 9.3 grams. [49]

Steam Power Systems of San Diego, California has also made progress on its bus. Incorporating a six cylinder engine (compound expansion type) and a new boiler and burner, the generating unit shows "increased efficiency and good economy." Company General Manager Richard Burtz says:

> The burner-boiler or convection bank, has a burner at one end, similar to jet engine burners. The hot gas is then flowed over the convection bank which is primarily made of stainless steel tubing. The intake air and fuel and so forth are brought into the boiler. In our particular case, we have fans incorporated right into the boiler. Another feature is that it has an air-cooled outer case . . . It is a very safe type of boiler. There is no large energy storage. [50]

This steam generating unit is capable of 240 horsepower at 2,100 r.p.m. with 825 foot-pounds pressure.[51] It is presently undergoing further improvement and should be important in the race to develop a pollution free engine.

Today's engineers already have a good idea as to what the

modern steam car will be like. It would possess a small steam or flourocarbon generating unit, a turbine or piston engine, or some combination of each and a compact burner capable of accepting kerosene or gasoline. It would be silent and powerful, and with its unique torque characteristics it should possess good pickup and good engine braking power. Powerful reverse torque would be available at all times for non-fade high speed braking—a life-saving feature at highway speeds or in hilly country.[52] Such cars would also be open to innovation in design and could have an engine for each wheel, an especially advantageous feature for utility vehicles. The modern steam car would also be long lasting. With an engine that operates at a slow rate of r.p.m.s, a lifespan of from 200,000 to 300,0000 miles would be common.[53] The steam generating unit would have fewer components and be less complex than its internal combustion counterparts. As the starting principle is entirely different drivers would not have to put up with a battery. Lights, radio and other accessories would receive power from an alternator, which can be run from the main engine or, where this is not possible, from a small auxiliary engine. A rheostat or other governing device could maintain an even current. Being non-polluting it could be idled in closed areas. This feature would save thousands of lives which are lost by asphyxiation caused by carbon monoxide from gas cars.

Steam cars should be cheap to purchase. Discussing his own car, scientist Wallace Minto says,

> These automobiles, in mass production, will weigh about the same or slightly less than a comparable car today. They will be cheaper by a couple of hundred dollars and get the same mileage on kerosene as the new auto does on gasoline.[54]

Overall operating costs should also be less. There is very little crankcase oil to change, no oil filter to change, no complicated air pollution controls or any of the other necessities associated with gas cars. Tire wear will be less because of uniform power delivery to all wheels. Thus high repair costs, incompetent mechanics and long waits at crowded garages would become memories.

The question asked now is whether the American auto makers are ready to adopt steam. Their answer is a qualified no. *The Report of the President's Task Force on Air Pollution* states:

> The initial enthusiasm for the steam engine as a low-pollution replacement for the gasoline engine has dwindled. However, further development of the steam engine (or Rankine cycle) should not be abandoned.[55]

In place of steam Detroit has considered a number of alternatives. The Wankel engine presently seems to be the most likely candidate for the immediate future.[56] Developed before the Second World War by German auto engineer Felix Wankel, the engine operates on a totally new principle. A spinning rotor, used instead of conventional pistons, opens and closes valves through the process of intake, compression, ignition and exhaust.[57] The little rotary engine is particularly attractive because it has few moving parts and is cheap to manufacture. Its biggest drawbacks have been leaky seals, lack of durability, engine hot spots and high emissions.[58] The latter problem is supposed to be solvable because large air-pollution control equipment can be added under the hood next to the small seventy cubic inch engine.

A Japanese built Mazda RX2 coupe equipped with such an engine was compared with a 1972 Ford Torino in a recent test conducted by an independent consumer testing organization.[59] The findings showed serious faults with the car's air-pollution control equipment. With eleven valves and controls plus "a thermal reactor in the exhaust system," it is too complicated to be effective.[60] Consumers' Union stated that "the smog-controlled Mazda Wankel isn't as clean burning as some sources have claimed."[61] In fact several large 1972 V-8 automobiles were better able to comply with the government's emission standards.[62]

Once again Detroit is gambling on a dark horse, with many questions left unanswered. What if the Wankel's faults cannot be corrected? What can be done to correct the starting and stalling problems associated with sophisticated pollution controls? What will happen if leaded gas or some unwanted additive gets into an advanced pollution control system? What can be done to halt the expected price increase in cars equipped with expensive pollution controls?

An attempt to correct the pollution problem by removing lead from gasoline has proved a failure. *Automotive News* reported that "tiny amounts of lead will probably be found for several years in unleaded gasoline and this could prove troublesome for the catalytic converters designed to clean up automobile emissions."[63]

General Motors claims its catalytic converter can eliminate 95 per cent of carbon monoxide and hydrocarbon emissions.[64] Costing approximately $300 and resembling a muffler, this device would be positioned forward of the conventional muffler. Such converters, however, have not been perfected, rely on lead free gas and are expensive to manufacture and maintain.

Automobiles operated on propane have been heralded as a final solution to the problem. The latest evidence, however, proves otherwise. First of all, conversion of a standard-size internal combustion-powered car to such a fuel system costs just under $500, an expensive venture.[65] The driver will still get approximately the same miles per gallon, although it has been reported that "some users experience a decline in mileage of 5% to 10%."[66] After adding a high-pressure storage tank, a fuelock strainer, a pressure-reducing converter and a special manifold to his vehicle, the driver will pay 50¢ and up for propane fuel, provided such fuel is readily available in his area. Supply outlets are presently quite limited. Granted there was sufficient petroleum, a mass conversion to L-P (Liquified-Petroleum) gas or a mass production of L-P vehicles could prove catastrophic for the petroleum industry because there are not enough trucks to supply L-P throughout the nation. Furthermore, L-P gas vehicles will not meet 1976 Environmental Protection Act standards.[67]

There are many who still favor the gasoline turbine-powered car, which had its chance in 1954. Long a favorite of Chrysler Corporation, which distributed 200 such cars for testing throughout the country, it has proved a flop.[68] Although turbine engines cost "less to maintain" than their piston engine counterparts, they lack pickup power and good fuel economy.[69] According to the Chrysler Corporation, "to be economical [it] must operate at high temperatures of up to 3,000 degrees Fahrenheit at which oxygen reacts with nitrogen, causing the engine to emit nitrogen oxide."[70] The turbine cannot meet current E.P.A. standards and for Chrysler to switch to such an engine would, said George Huebner, director of research, cost the company "one billion dollars."[71]

The Ford Motor Company is betting on many engines, including the 143 year old Stirling engine.[72] Called the "hot air engine" because it uses hot gases (which are later cooled) to move a piston in a cylinder, it is quite similar to a reciprocating steam engine, especially in its combustion of a fuel in a burner.[73] Ford and the Dutch electronics firm, N.V. Philips Company, have reached a multimillion dollar agreement to develop the engine. In the past the problem with the Stirling has been size and complexity; General Motors dropped it after spending millions to improve its pollution and performance characteristics.[74] According to the *Wall Street Journal* "There was no indication at Ford, however, that the Stirling development would take precedence over other engines that it is working on. Nor was there any hint that Ford was backing off its Wankel research in favor of Stirling."[75] In fact Ford is seriously interested in steam engines. *Automotive News* states that "since the spring of 1970, Ford Motor Company has had a four million dollar commitment to Thermo Electron, along with a two million dollar investment by the company itself, plus funds from the Environmental Protection Agency ($1,082,900), the Rockefeller Family Fund and Boston's Street Investment Company."[76] Thermo Electron has not disappointed its backers as it has developed a Rankine cycle engine using "an organic fluid for internal expansion." In a Rankine cycle system an enclosed fluid is heated to expansion in a boiler and later condensed into a liquid, being continuously recycled by a pump. Henry Ford II was so impressed that he visited the Waltham, Massachusetts firm to verify in person the favorable reports he has received the past two years.[77] He found that Thermo Electron's engines could easily meet the present Environmental Protection Act pollution standards. Such engines can be built with readily available materials using ordinary techniques, and several were to be installed in full-sized Ford cars in the fall of 1973.[78]

After eighty years electrics are still unable to compete with steam and gas cars. After years of research the very best electric car is "limited to approximately 75 miles on a charge and a speed of 60 m.p.h."[79] One electric vehicle designer has said:

> If you want an electric vehicle to travel over 50 m.p.h., the cost of the drive system can be three times that of a 30 m.p.h. vehicle. In a conventional car an increase in engine size does not greatly increase the cost of the power plant, but in the electric vehicle you pay a premium for the horsepower and speed.[80]

The 30 m.p.h. electric vehicle, little more than a spruced-up golf cart, runs close to $2,000 and costs 21¢ to recharge after traveling from 40 to 60 miles.[81] Its use will probably be severely restricted because of its speed and size. A battery capable of storing vast amounts of energy for long periods has not been developed. The silver-zinc, nickel-cadmium, lithium-halide and lithium-chloride batteries have short life-spans and are quite expensive. Until an effective battery and a new electric motor to handle such a battery are made, the electric car will not be a serious contender in the race to displace the internal combustion engine.

Recently there has been much talk of diesel engines being able to solve the pollution problem. Coming in a variety of shapes and sizes, the diesel engine commonly used in smaller automobiles by Daimler-Benz of Germany is a 134 cubic-inch four-cylinder motor generating sixty horsepower.[82] According to Rudolph Uhlenhaut, Director of Passenger Car Development for the company, such an engine operates when,

> in the moment of maximum compression, fuel is injected into the precombustion chamber, which is connected with the main combustion chamber cylinder. The temperature of the highly compressed air exceeds the self-ignition point of diesel fuel. Rising pressure pushes the contents of the precombustion chamber through staggered openings in the cylinder.[83]

The diesel has many advantages over the internal-combustion

engine, especially in its ability to burn a cheaper fuel and get more miles per gallon. Mr. Uhlenhaut is unhappy to report, however, that "the present diesel engine even with presently known modifications does not meet the 1976 NOx standard. In fact it exceeds the standard by about three times more than the standard would permit."[84] This factor alone eliminates the diesel as a replacement for the gas car.

On the other hand, foreign auto makers Honda and Fiat have boasted that their compound vortex controlled combustion (stratified charge) engine can meet the amended E.P.A. standards.[85]

The new Honda engine is similar to a four-stroke gasoline engine except that it has a small combustion chamber designed around each spark plug and two small "intake valves fitted to each cylinder."[86] The engine still needs refinement and according to Detroit "engine specialists" the compound vortex controlled combustion engine is a poor performer and a big gas eater.[87]

With advances in space age technology some have claimed that fuel cells and atomic power are the answer to the pollution problem. Work with such energy sources, however, is too theoretical and impractical to consider for passenger cars. Both are dangerous, bulky and expensive and require much research to perfect.

With the mass of evidence favoring steam again, with the lessons learned from the failure of the first steam cars still fresh in the minds of inventors, with energy shortages and pollution of the air so critical everywhere, crisis is at last being faced. In the words of *Automotive News,* "it is time that the nation took stock of itself and where it is going. Who has a clear idea of U.S. priorities? Of how we can make the most of strengths and offset our weaknesses."[88] There is little hope of a breakthrough in the development of efficient air pollution controls for the internal combustion engine car. Propane-equipped cars or diesel engine cars cannot solve the problem. Charles M. Heinen, in charge of Chrysler Corporation's pollution control program, says: "The answer to the question, Are we ready for the 1975 emission standards? is a resounding no."[89] General Motors president Edward M. Cole states that 1975 standards can be met "only with prototype systems in experimental cars at low mileage. Much progress is required to get from these carefully tuned experimental systems to mass-produced hardware that not only functions properly in the hands of our customers, but also meets the federal requirements."[90] It must be kept in mind that E.P.A. standards require a car's pollution control system to last "five years or 50,000 miles." At present "the best systems have met the standards for only 15,000 miles." Continued use of the gas car in large urban areas can only lead to disaster. John Maga, Director of the California State Air Resources Board says that to meet the oxidant standard "might require an 80 per cent traffic reduction." In an area such as Los Angeles "it would mean virtual paralysis of economic and social life in the region, as it would in most other communities."[91] The steam car can meet E.P.A. standards quickly. It can restore decently breathable air to us at long last. The steam car also makes it possible to cleanse the atmosphere of dangerous noise levels; and by its ability to use all kinds of cheap and readily available fuels— kerosene, alcohols, coal gas and coal—make us independent of the energy crises that continue to threaten us. We have one choice—steam cars or no cars.

Appendices

Steam Cars Manufactured in the United States
1860-present

American 1900-1903
American 1922
Artzberger
Aultman
Austin
Auto-Loco
Baker
Baldwin
Ball
Battin
Best
Binney-Burnham
Boss
Brecht
Bristol
Bryan
Cameron
Cannon
Capitol
Century
Cincinnati
Clark

Clermont
Coats
Conrad
Cotta
Crompton
Crouch
Darling
Delling
Detroit
Doble
Dudgeon
Duryea
Eastman
Eclipse
Elberon
Elite
Empire
Endurance
Essex
Federal
Field
Foster

Friedman
Gaeth
Gearless
Geneva
Geni
Grout
Hartley
Henrietta
Hess
Hoffman
Holland
Holyoke
House
Howard
Hudson
Hyde
International
Jaxon
Jenkins
Johnson
Keene
Kellogg

Kensington
Keystone
Kidder
Kraft

Lane
Lane Wagon
Leach
Lear
Locke
Locomobile
Loomis
Lutz
Lyons

Malden
Mason
McKay
Mechaley
Mercury
Meteor
Mills
Milwaukee
Minto
Mobile
Morse

New England

Ofeldt
Ormond
Overholt
Overman
Oxford

Pawtucket
Peerless
Porter
Prescott
Puritan

Randall
Randolph
Reading
Remel-Vincent
Rogers
Ross

Simons
Skene
Spencer
Springer
Springfield
Squier
Standard
Stanley
Stanton

Steamobile
Stearns
Sterling
Storck
Strathmore
Stringer
Strouse
Sunset
Super-Steamer
Taunton
Terwilliger
Thompson
Toledo
Tractmobile
Trask-Detroit
Trinity
Victor
Waltham
Watson
Watt Steam
Webb Jay
Westfield
White
Whitney
Williams
Wood-Loco

The United States government is attempting to apply today's technology to Rankine Cycle systems. The government must be sure that the technology is such that it can meet 1976 emission standards and that various problems associated with Rankine Cycle systems can be solved—*e.g.*, that the size of condensers can be reduced. A number of firms submitted competitive bids to conduct research or build components necessary to determine the workability of four Rankine Cycle systems: (1) steam working in a reciprocating expander; (2) steam working in a turbine expander; (3) organic fluid working in a reciprocating expander; (4) organic fluid working in a turbine expander. All four systems are still being evaluated and reports are issued monthly.

The following firms are funded by the E.P.A.

Paxve Inc.
840 Production Place
Newport Beach, California 92660

Monsanto Company
800 N. Linberg Blvd.
St. Louis, Missouri 63166

General Electric Corp.
570 Lexington Avenue
New York, New York 10022

Steam Engine Systems
570 Pleasant Street
Watertown, Massachusetts 02172

Thermo Electron Corp.
101 First Avenue
Waltham, Massachusetts 02154

Chandler-Evans
(Div. of Colt Industries)
Charter Oak Blfd.
West Hartford, Conn. 06101

Aerojet Liquid Rocket
Highway 500 and Aerojet Road
Sacramento, California 95801

Garrett Air Research Corp.
6201 West Imperial Highway
Los Angeles, California 90053

Battelle Memorial Institute
505 King Avenue
Columbus, Ohio 43216

Marquardt Corp.
16555 Saticoy
Van Nuys, California 91406

Solar Corp.
2200 Pacific Highway
San Diego, California 92101

University of Michigan
Ann Arbor, Michigan 48103

Notes

I /Early Adventures With Self-propelled Vehicles

1. Dr. A.J. Haagen-Smit to the President of the United States, June 9, 1970, the President's Task Force on Air Pollution, *Cleaner Air for the Nation* (Washington D.C.: U.S. Government Printing Office, 1970), II.

2. *Ibid.*

3. *Alternatives to the Gasoline-Powered Internal Combustion Engine* Hearing Before the Panel on Environmental Science and Technology of the Subcommittee on Air and Water Pollution of the Committee on Public Works United States Senate, Ninety-Second Congress, March 14, 1972, p. 73.

4. *Facts on File* Vol. XXXI, No. 1595, (May 13-19, 1971), p. 373.

5. *New York Times*, January 14, 1973, p. 35.

6. Scientific Analysis Corporation, *Steam Bus Symposium Proceedings, November 17, 1971* (Washington D.C.: Urban Mass Transportation Administration, 1971), p. 24.

7. *Ibid.*

8. Robert H. Thurston, *A History of the Growth of the Steam Engine* (New York: D. Appleton Co., 1897), p. 13; H.W. Dickinson, *A Short History of the Steam Engine* (Cambridge: University Press, 1938), p. 5.

9. Thurston, *Growth of the Steam Engine*, p. 16.

10. *Ibid.*, p. 17; Herbert O. Duncan, *The World on Wheels* 2 Vols., (Paris: H.O. Duncan, 1926), I, p. 76.

11. Thurston, *Growth of the Steam Engine*, pp. 20-21; John Timbs, *Wonderful Inventions* (London: George Routledge, 1867), p. 197.

12. Thurston, *Growth of the Steam Engine*, pp. 20-21.

13. Jean Duhalde, *A Description of the Empire of China and Chinese Tartary together with Korea and Tibet*, 2 vols., (London: T. Gardiner, 1738), II, p. 17; Paul Hasluck, *The Automobile* (London: Cassell Company, 1904), p. 46; Rhys Jenkins, *Motor Cars* (London: T. Unwin Fisher, 1902), p. 42.

14. Timbs, *Wonderful Inventions*, p. 192; Jenkins, *Motor Cars* p. 42.

15. Jenkins, *Motor Cars*, p. 42; Duncan, *World on Wheels* I, p. 81.

16. Timbs, *Wonderful Inventions*, p. 203.

17. A. Wolf, *A History of Science, Technology and Philosophy in the 16th and 17th Centuries* (New York: Macmillan, 1935), pp. 235-242.

18. Timbs, *Wonderful Inventions*, p. 203.

19. Jenkins, *Motor Cars*, p. 43.

20. Timbs, *Wonderful Inventions*, pp. 204-205.

21. Thurston, *Growth of the Steam Engine*, p. 40.

22. L.T.C. Rolt, *Thomas Newcomen* (New York: August Kelley, 1968), pp. 98-101; Timbs, *Wonderful Inventions*, p. 204; In the Newcomen engine steam power was only used to equalize the pressure of the atmosphere and thus it was necessary to add the weight and heavy beam.

23. Rolt, *Thomas Newcomen*, p. 139.

24. H.W. Dickinson, *A Short History of the Steam Engine*, p. 66; Timbs, *Wonderful Inventions*, pp. 214-216.

25. H.W. Dickinson, *A Short History of the Steam Engine* pp. 83-85; H.W. Dickinson, Rhys Jenkins, *James Watt and the Steam Engine* (Oxford: Clarendon Press, 1927), pp. 123-125.

26. Commissioners of Patents for Inventions, *Abridgements of Specifications Relating to the Steam Engine* 2 Vols., (London: Eyre and Spottiswoode, 1871), I, 81.

27. Luke Herbert, *The Engineer's and Mechanic's Encyclopaedia, comprehending practical illustrations of the machinery and processes employed in every description of manufacture of the British Empire* 2 Vols. (London: Thomas Kelley, 1836), II, pp. 386-387.

28. *Ibid.*, p. 387.

29. Jenkins, *Motor Cars*, p. 53.

30. Pierre Souvestre, *Histoire de L'Automobile* (Paris: J. Dumoulin, 1907), pp. 18-20; M.F. Malepeyre, *Le Technologiste ou Archives de Progress de L'Industrie Francais et Etrangere* (Paris: Librarie Encyclopedique de Roret, 1867), pp. 42-45.

31. L.N. Roland to the Minister of War, January 23, 1801, Souvestre, *Histoire de L'Automobile*, p. 19.

32. *Ibid.*, p. 32.

33. *Ibid.*, pp. 22-24; Duncan, *World on Wheels*, I, p. 101.

34. Souvestre, *Histoire de L'Automobile*, p. 22.

35. Jenkins, *Motor Cars*, p. 49.

36. *Ibid.*

37. *Ibid.*

38. Alexander Gordon, *A Treatise Upon Elemental Locomotion and Interior Communication Wherein are Explained and Illustrated the history, practice and prospects of steam carriages*, Third Edition, (London: Thomas Tegg, 1836), p. 35.

39. Jenkins, *Motor Cars*, pp. 52-53.

40. *Ibid.*

41. Francis Tevithick, *Life of Richard Trevithick* 2 vols., (London: W.J. Welch, 1872), I, p. 71-72.

42. H.W. Dickinson, Arthur Titley, *Richard Trevithick, The Engineer and the Man* (Cambridge: The University Press, 1934), p. 52; The authors claim this vehicle was later destroyed by fire.

43. *Ibid.*, pp. 56-59; Commissioners of Patents, *Specifications of Patents*, II, p. 599.

44. Trevithick, *Life of Richard Trevithick*, I, p. 235; Dickinson, Titley, *Richard Trevithick, Engineer*, pp. 65-67.

45. Dickinson, Titley, *Richard Trevithick, Engineer*, pp. 107-108; Thurston, *Growth of the Steam Engine*, p. 175.

46. R.W. Kidner, *The First Hundred Road Motors* (London: Oakwood Press, 1950), p. 9.

47. *Ibid.*, p. 9; Herbert, *Engineer's and Mechanic's Encyclopaedia*, p. 450; Thurston, *Growth of the Steam Engine*, p. 10; Francis Maceroni, *Expositions and Illustrations Interesting to all those concerned in Steam Power, whether as applied to railroads, common roads, or to sea and inland navigation* (London: Effingham, Wilson, Royal Exchange, 1835), p. 67.

48. Herbert, *Engineer's and Mechanic's Encyclopaedia*, p. 450; L. Holley, Charles F.T. Young, C.E. and J.K. Fisher, *The Economy of Steam Power on Common Roads, with its History and Practice in Great Britain and its*

Progress in the United States (London: Atchley and Company, 1861), p. 34.

49. Herbert, *Engineer's and Mechanic's Encyclopaedia*, p. 450.

50. *Ibid.*,

51. *Ibid.*, p. 460.

52. Thurston, *Growth of the Steam Engine*, p. 162; Holley, Fisher, Young, *Economy of Steam Power on Common Roads*, p. 185.

53. Thurston, *Growth of the Steam Engine*, p. 165.

54. Gordon, *Treatise on Elemental Locomotion*, p. 31.

55. *Ibid.*,; Kidner, *The First Hundred Road Motors*, p. 31.

56. Maceroni, *Expositions and Illustrations*, p. 72.

57. Gordon, *Treatise on Elemental Locomotion*, p. 65.

58. *Ibid.*, pp. 66-67; John G. Carteret, "The First Motor Ride," *Automobile*, Vol. I (November 1, 1899), pp. 146-147.

59. Duncan, *World on Wheels*, I, pp. 120-121; Walter Hancock, *Narrative of Twelve Years Experiments* (London: J. Weale, 1838), p. 36; Herbert, *Engineer's and Mechanic's Encyclopaedia*, p. 492.

60. Hancock, *Narrative of Twelve Years*, p. 23; Duncan, *World on Wheels*, I, p. 121.

61. Herbert, *Engineer's and Mechanic's Encyclopaedia*, p. 487.

62. Maceroni, *Expositions and Illustrations*, p. 76; In the oscillating engine the cylinder performs a swinging motion when receiving steam.

63. Commissioners of Patents, *Specifications Relating to the Steam Engine*, I, p. 272.

64. Herbert, *Engineer's and Mechanic's Encyclopaedia*, p. 489.

65. *Ibid.*, p. 494.

66. Hancock, *Narrative of Twelve Years*, p. 22; Kidner, *The First Hundred Road Motors*, p. 16.

67. Thurston, *Growth of the Steam Engine*, p. 169; Herbert, *Engineer's and Mechanic's Encyclopaedia*, p. 566.

68. Gordon, *Treatise on Elemental Locomotion*, p. 82.

69. *Ibid.*

70. *Ibid.*; Thurston, *Growth of the Steam Engine*, p. 171.

71. Maceroni, *Expositions and Illustrations*, pp. 30-31.

72. Gordon, *Treatise on Elemental Locomotion*, p. 36.

73. *Ibid.*, p. 82.

74. Maceroni, *Expositions and Illustrations*, pp. 10, 35.

75. Hancock, *Narrative of Twelve Years*, pp. 36, 86.

76. House of Commons *Report on Steam Carriages by the Select Committee* (Washington D.C.: Reprinted as Document 101, 22nd Congress, First Session, House of Representatives, 1832), p. 15.

77. Gordon, *Treatise on Elemental Locomotion*, pp. 83-84; Maceroni, *Expositions and Illustrations*, pp. 94-95.

78. Gordon, *Treatise on Elemental Locomotion*, p. 84.

79. *Ibid.*, p. 97; Kidner, *The First Hundred Road Motors*, p. 28.

80. Kidner, *The First Hundred Road Motors*, p. 28.

81. *House of Commons Report*, pp. 17, 18, 20, 128; Thurston, *Growth of the Steam Engine*, p. 171.

82. Petition of Goldsworthy Guerney to the House of Commons, April 29, 1834; Maceroni, *Expositions and Illustrations*, pp. 109-111.

83. *Ibid.*, pp. 18-19; 109.

84. Kidner, *The First Hundred Road Motors*, p. 22.

85. Holley, Fisher, Young, *The Economy of Steam Power on Common Roads*, p. 186.

86. Kidner, *The First Hundred Road Motors*, p. 25.

87. *Ibid.*

88. *Ibid.*, p. 36.

89. *Ibid.*, p. 37.

90. Duncan, *World on Wheels*, I, p. 171.

91. In the flash boiler pure water is sprayed on red hot metallic surfaces and is instantly converted to steam. The Englishman John Payne was granted a patent on such a boiler in 1736, but it was not actually used until 1827.

II/Backyard Tinkers

1. Carroll W. Pursell, *Early Stationary Steam Engines in America* (Washington, D.C.: Smithsonian Institution Press, 1969), p. 10.

2. *Ibid.*, p. 6.

3. John L. Bishop, *A History of American Manufactures* 3 vols., (New York: Augustus Kelley, 1966), I, p. 547; William Nelson, *Josiah Hornblower and the First Steam Engine in America* (Newark: Daily Advertiser Printing House, 1883), p. 9.

4. Bishop, *History of American Manufactures* I, p. 534; Carl Bridenbaugh, *The Colonial Craftsman* (Chicago: University of Chicago Press, 1950), p. 85.

5. Bishop, *History of American Manufactures*, I, p. 534.

6. *Ibid.*, I, p. 761.

7. Grenville and Dorothy Bathe, *Oliver Evans, A Chronicle of Early American Engineering* (Philadelphia: Historical Society of Pennsylvania, 1935), p. 6.

8. Oliver Evans, *The Young Steam Engineers Guide* (Philadelphia: Carey and Lea, 1824), p. 6.

9. David Read, *Life of Nathan Read* (New York: Hurd and Houghton, 1870), pp. 5-7.

10. *Ibid.*, p. 87.

11. Newton C. Brainard, "Apollos Kinsley," *Connecticut Historical Society Bulletin* Vol. XXVI (January, 1961), pp. 12-20; Forest Morgan, *Connecticut as Colony and State* (Hartford: The Publishing Society of Connecticut, 1904), p. 267; J. Hammond Trumbull (ed.), *Memorial History of Hartford County, Connecticut*, 2 vols. (Boston: Edward Osgood, 1886), I, p. 569.

12. Roger Burlingame, *March of the Iron Men* (New York: Grosset and Dunlop, 1938), p. 181.

13. Dirk J. Struik, *Yankee Science in the Making* (New York: Collier Books, 1962), p. 304; Frederick Graff, "Notice of the Earliest Steam Engines Used in the United States," *Journal of the Franklin Institute*, Vol. LV (October, 1853), p. 207.

14. Bishop, *History of American Manufactures*, I, p. 732.

15. Bathe, *Oliver Evans*, p. 49; Evans, *Steam Engineers Guide*, pp. 50-51.

16. Evans, *Steam Engineers Guide*, pp. 50-51.

17. Bathe, *Oliver Evans*, p. 109; *Relf's Philadelphia Gazette*, July 13, 1805, p. 1.

18. Pursell, *Early Stationary Steam Engines in America*, p. 47.

19. Evans, *Steam Engineers Guide*, p. 50.

20. *Ibid.*, p. 50.

21. *Ibid.*

22. *Ibid.*; Bathe, *Oliver Evans*, pp. 99-100.

23. Evans, *Steam Engineers Guide*, p. 53.

24. Struik, *Yankee Science in the Making*, pp. 312, 315.

25. Robert F. Scott, "That Walking, Puffing Devil, An Almanac of Steam Engines," *Automobile Quarterly*, Vol. II, (Summer, 1963), p. 154.

26. Holley, Fisher, Young, *Steam on Common Roads*, p. 349.

27. *Ibid.*, p. 530.

28. *Ibid.*

29. *Ibid.*, p. 350.

30. *Ibid.*

31. Lyman H. Weeks, *Automobile Biographies* (New York: Monograph Press, 1904), p. 153; American Institute, *Transactions of the American Institute* (Albany: Charles Van Benthuysen, 1858), p. 631.

32. Holley, Fisher, Young, *The Economy of Steam Power on Common*

Roads pp. 352-353; *Transactions of the American Institute*, p. 631.

33. *Brochure of the American Steam Carriage Company, 1851* (New York: J.P. Prall, 1851), p. 2.

34. James Allen (ed.), *Digest of United States Automobile Patents 1789-July, 1900* (Washington, D.C.: H.B. Russell, 1900), p. 481.

35. Peter Temin, *The Jacksonian Economy* (New York: Norton 1969), pp. 139-141.

36. *Hunt's Merchants' Magazine* Vol. XXV, (September, 1851), pp. 381-382.

37. Joseph A. Durrenberger, *Turnpikes, A Study of the Toll Road Movement in the Middle Atlantic States and Maryland* (Valdosta, Georgia: Southern Stationer and Printing Co., 1931), pp. 145-146.

38. George R. Taylor, *The Transportation Revolution, 1815-1860* Volume IV of *The Economic History of the United States* (New York: Harper and Row, 1951), pp. 16-17.

39. Holley, Fisher, Young, *The Economy of Steam Power on Common Roads*, p. 353; Thurston, *Growth of the Steam Engine*, p. 360; P.R. Hodge was the first American to construct a self-propelled fire engine, but it was too heavy for rapid transportation. The Hodge and Fisher fire engines were built at the Novelty Iron Works, New York City.

40. Robert F. Scott, "Richard Dudgeon, Machinist," *Automobile Quarterly*, Vol. V (Winter, 1967), p. 251.

41. *Ibid.*, p. 254; Duncan, *World on Wheels*, II, p. 911.

42. Robert F. Scott, *Automobile Quarterly*, Vol. V, p. 254.

43. *Ibid.*, p. 252.

44. *Ibid.*: Duncan, *World on Wheels*, II, p. 911.

45. Duncan, *World on Wheels*, II, p. 911: *New York Mail and Express* November 9, 1900, p. 5.

46. Reynold Wik, *Steam Power on the American Farm* (Philadelphia: The University Press, 1953), p. 61.

47. *Ibid.*

48. *Ibid.*

49. *Ibid.*

50. J.B. Irvine, "A Steam Wagon Invented by an Early Resident of South Dakota," *South Dakota Historical Collections* Vol. X (1921) pp. 370-371.

51. *Ibid.*, p. 371.

52. *Ibid.*

53. *Ibid.*, p. 375.

54. Joseph Brown to Colonel Samuel Brown, November 30, 1869, *Ibid.*, p. 380.

55. *Ibid.*

56. Wik, *Steam Power on the American Farm*, p. 66.

57. *Ibid.*, p. 67.

58. *Ibid.*

59. *Moorhead Advocate* (Moorhead, Minn.) October 13, 1877, p. 2.

60. Alan Nevins, Frank Hill, *Ford, The Times, The Man, The Company* (New York: Charles Scribners, 1954), pp. 54-55.

61. Thurston, *Growth of the Steam Engine*, p. 352; Park Benjamin (ed.), *Appleton's Cyclopedia of Applied Mechanics* (New York: D. Appleton Company, 1879), p. 626.

62. George W. Browne, *The Amoskeag Manufacturing Company, A History* (Manchester: Amoskeag Manufacturing Company, 1915), p. 79.

63. George Woodbury, *The Story of a Stanley Steamer* (Los Angeles: Clymer Publications, 1967), p. 83; Springfield *Republican* November 10, 1872; *New York Times*, November 10, 1872, p. 1.

64. *New Hampshire Sunday News* (Manchester), August 16, 1964, p. 4; Benjamin, *Appleton's Cyclopedia*, p. 631; George Woodbury, *Story of a Stanley Steamer*, p. 85.

65. Benjamin, *Appleton's Cyclopedia*, p. 626.

66. Woodbury, *Story of a Stanley Steamer*, p. 85.

67. Captain Cordier, "The Horseless Fire Engine," *Automobile* Vol. I (December, 1899), p. 230.

68. Browne, *Amoskeag Manufacturing Company*, p. 80.

69. *Scientific American* Vol. XXI (March 14, 1863), p. 34; *Lowell Daily News*, August 8, 1863, p. 1; William H. Austin, also of Lowell, assisted Roper in developing this vehicle.

70. *Automobile* Vol. XVIII (March 1, 1917), pp. 466-470; *Valley Gleaner* (Lee, Mass.) October 13, 1863, p. 3; Smith H. Oliver, Donald H. Berkebile, *The Smithsonian Collection of Automobiles and Motorcycles* (Washington, D.C.: Smithsonian Institution Press, 1968), pp. 12-13.

71. *Scientific American* Vol. XXI (November 28, 1863), p. 51.

72. *Ibid.*, p. 52.

73. Oliver, Berkebile, *The Smithsonian Collection of Automobiles*, pp. 24-25.

74. *Journal* (Racine, Wisc.), May 7, 1863 p. 1; *Horseless Age* Vol. XI (January 14, 1903), p. 63.

75. *Journal* (Racine) May 7, 1873, p. 3.

76. *Journal-News*, (Racine, Wisc.), May 21, 1921, p. 16; S.E. Austin, "Wisconsin's First Motor Car was a Product of 1871," *Motor Age* Vol. XXV (March 19, 1914), pp. 13-14; *Scientific American* Vol. XXXIV (January 9, 1876), p. 64.

77. *Journal-News*, (Racine), May 21, 1921, pp. 16-17; Frank Cetin, "The Father of the Automobile," *Wisconsin Tales and Trails* (Summer, 1963), p. 13.

78. Cetin, *Wisconsin Tales and Trails*, p. 13; *The Wisconsin Magazine* (November/December, 1924), p. 17; *Laws of Wisconsin*, March 5, 1875, chapter 134, p. 233.

79. *The Wisconsin Magazine*, p. 17.

80. *Journal*, (Racine, Wisc.), July 19, 1876, p. 1.

81. *Ibid.*, September 2, 1878, p. 1.

82. Allen, *Digest of U.S. Automobile Patents*, p. 1-488.

83. State of New York, *Ninth Annual Report of the Factory Inspectors of the State of New York* (Albany: J.B. Lyon, 1895), p. 833.

84. State of New York, *Thirteenth Annual Report of the Factory Inspectors of the State of New York* (New York: Wynkoop, Hallenback and Crawford, 1899), p. 12.

85. Ralph N. Hill, *Sidewheeler Saga* (New York: Rinehart and Company, 1953), p. 96.

86. *Ibid.*, p. 97.

87. *Ibid.*, p. 100.

88. *Ibid.*

89. *New York Times*, June 16, 1904, p. 1.

90. "An Interview with R.E. Olds," *The Bulb Horn* Vol. X (October, 1942), p. 4.

91. *Ibid.*, p. 4.

92. *Scientific American* Vol. LXVI (May 21, 1892), p. 329.

93. *Ibid.*

94. Glenn A. Niemeyer, *The Automotive Career of Ransom E. Olds* (East Lansing, Michigan: Michigan State University Press, 1963), p. 9.

95. Ransom E. Olds, "The Horseless Carriage," *The Michigan Engineers Annual 1898*, p. 90.

96. Duncan, *World on Wheels*, I, p. 389.

97. John B. Rae, *The American Automobile A Brief History* (Chicago: University of Chicago Press, 1965), p. 3.

98. "Brayton's Early Work in Oil Motors," *Horseless Age* Vol. XII (November 25, 1903), p. 560.

99. Dugald Clark, *The Gas Engine* second edition, (New York: Appletons, 1887), p. 139; *Scientific American Supplement* I, (May 27, 1876), p. 339. Further experimentation proved that the Brayton engine was not economical.

100. *Scientific American Supplement* Vol. I (May 27, 1876), p. 339.

101. *Ibid.*

102. *Scientific American* Vol. LXVII (November 26, 1892), p. 1; Tube-timers consisted of an incandescent tube encased in a larger tube which was lined with asbestos.

103. *Ibid.*

104. Hiram P. Maxim, *Horseless Carriage Days* (New York: Dover, 1962), p. 47.

105. Diagram and description dated August 15, 1895, Hiram P. Maxim Collection, Connecticut State Library.

106 *New York Times*, April 19, 1896, p. 28.

107. Felicien Michotte, "The Electric Automobile," *Automobile* Vol. I (November, 1899), p. 186.

108. L.T.C. Rolt, *Motoring History* (New York: E.P. Dutton, 1964), p. 33.

109. *Ibid.*, p. 23; Hasluck, *The Automobile*, p. 765.

110. *The Motocycle* Vol. I (May, 1896), p. 10.

111. *Horseless Age* Vol. I (November, 1895), p. 7.

112. *Ibid.*, pp. 52-53; *Chicago Times-Herald*, November 29, 1895; p. 1; W.H. McIntyre, "America's First Horseless Carriage Road Race," *Motor Age*, Vol. XXIV (August 7, 1913), pp. 18-19.

113. *Chicago Times-Herald* November 29, 1895, p. 1.

III/The Stanley, Locomobile and White

1. *Motor World* Vol. I (December 13, 1900), p. 7.

2. *Horseless Age* Vol. II (September, 1896), p. 6; Automobile Manufacturers Association, *Automobiles of America* (Detroit: Wayne State University Press, 1968), p. 17.

3. *Automobiles of America*, p. 17.

4. Nevins, Hill, *Ford*, p. 172.

5. *Automobiles of America*, pp. 179, 188-189.

6. *Motor World* Vol. I (December 13, 1900), p. 1.

7. *Horseless Age* Vol. IV (April 12, 1899), p. 11; Victor S. Clark, *History of Manufactures in the United States* 3 Vols. (New York: Peter Smith, 1949), I, p. 158; Maxim, *Horseless Carriage Days*, p. 150; These cabs were capable of traveling from twenty to thirty miles on one charge. Their speed was limited to twelve miles per hour, which was considered fast in its day.

8. *Horseless Age* Vol. I (December, 1896), p. 13.

9. "The First Practical Horseless Carriage," No author or publisher

listed, in the files of the Locomobile Company of America Collection, p. 3.

10. *Horseless Age* Vol. IV (September, 1899), p. 10.

11. Hugh Dolnar, "The Stanley Steam Wagons," *Cycle and Automobile Trade Journal* Vol. VIII (May, 1903), p. 52.

12. "The First Practical Horseless Carriage," pp. 3-4.

13. Thomas Derr, *The Modern Steam Car and its Background* (Los Angeles: Clymer Publications, 1951), p. 45.

14. Dolnar, *Cycle and Automobile Trade Journal*, Vol. VIII, p. 52.

15. *Ibid.*, p. 53.

16. Ray Stanley, "The Stanley Steamer," *Floyd Clymer's Historical Motor Scrapbook Steam Car Edition* (Los Angeles: Clymer Publications, 1946), p. 17.

17. *Ibid.*, p. 19.

18. Derr, *The Modern Steam Car*, p. 53; *The Steam Car* (official publication of the Stanley Motor Carriage Company) Vol. II, p. 2.

19. Derr, *The Modern Steam Car*, p. 53.

20. Advertisement of the Automobile Company of America, July, 1899, in the *Steam Automobile* Vol. III (Spring, 1966), p. 13.

21. Dolnar, *Cycle and Automobile Trade Journal*, Vol. VIII, p. 54.

22. *Horseless Age* Vol. VI (April 18, 1900), p. 25.

23. *Mobile Company of America*, 1900 brochure (Tarrytown, New York: Mobile Company, 1900), p. 2.

24. *Ibid.*

25. *Mobile Company of America*, 1903 brochure, (Tarrytown, New York: Mobile Company, 1903), pp. 7-9.

26. *Press-Record*, (Tarrytown, New York), August 3, 1901, p. 3.

27. *Boston Transcript*, November 8, 1900, p. 6.

28. *Mobile Company of America*, 1900 brochure, p. 9.

29. *Ibid.*

30. *Mobile Company of America* 1903 brochure, pp. 9-12.

31. Locomobile advertisement appearing in *Steam Automobile* Vol. VIII (Spring, 1966), p. 23.

32. *Locomobile Company of America*, 1900 brochure, (Bridgeport, Conn: Locomobile Company, 1900), p. 3.

33. Rudyard Kipling to the Editor of *McClures*, July 4, 1901, copy of autographed letter in the Automotive History Collection, Detroit Public Library.

34. Captain R.S. Walker to the Locomobile Company, August 10, 1901 *The Locomobile in War*, 1901 (Bridgeport: Locomobile Company, 1901), p. 5.

35. *The Locomobile Some Practical Tests*, 1900 brochure, (Bridgeport: Locomobile Company, 1900), p. 4.

36. *How to Operate the Locomobile*, 1903 pamphlet (Bridgeport: Locomobile Company, 1903), pp. 2-14.

37. *Locomobile Company of America*, 1903 brochure (Bridgeport: Locomobile, 1903), pp. 1-9.

38. *Locomobile Company of America* 1900 brochure pp. 9-14.

39. *Ibid.*

40. *Locomobile Company of America*, 1903 brochure pp. 8-9.

41. G. N. Georgano (ed.), *The Complete Encyclopaedia of Motorcars, 1885-1968* (London: Ebury Press, 1968), p. 349.

42. *Bridgeport Post*, April 17, 1927, p. 9.

43. *Horseless Age* Vol. V (December 6, 1899), p. 49; Vol. VII, (October 31, 1900), p. 8.

44. *Ibid.*, Vol. V (November 7, 1900), p. 47.

45. George Woodbury, *The Story of a Stanley Steamer* (Los Angeles: Clymer Publications, 1967), p. 174.

46. *Ibid.*, pp. 174-175.

47. Thomas Derr, *The Modern Steam Car*, p. 53.

48. Stanley Motor Carriage Company, *Announcement for 1916* (Newton, Massachusetts: Stanley Motor Carriage Co., 1916), p. 16.

49. Dolnar, *Cycle and Automobile Trade Journal* Vol. VIII, pp. 54-56.

50. *Ibid.*, p. 59-60.

51. Stanley Steam Cars, *1916 Season*, p. 15; *Floyd Clymer's Historical Motor Scrapbook, Steam Car Edition*, p. 127.

52. *Floyd Clymer's Historical Motor Scrapbook, Steam Car Edition*, p. 123.

53. Stanley Steam Cars, *1916 Season*, p. 15; A small plunger pump fed fuel to the main burner. Pressure was maintained in two quart-sized pressure tanks; there was no pressure in the main fuel tanks. Thus, when the filler cap was removed there was no loss of pressure.

54. Ray Stanley, "The Stanley Steamer," *Clymer's Motor Scrapbook*, p. 19.

55. Stanley Motor Carriage Company, *1908 Models* (Newton: Stanley Motor Carriage Company, 1908), pp. 2, 6, 7.

56. Carleton F. Stanley, "The Early History of the Stanley Company," *Floyd Clymer's Historical Motor Scrapbook, Steam Car Edition*, p. 24.

57. *Ibid.*

58. Ray W. Stanley, "Evaporating the Stanley Steamer Myth," *Automobile Quarterly* Vol. II (Summer, 1963), p. 123.

59. White Motors Corporation, *The Story of White Sewing Machines* (Cleveland: White Motors Corporation, 1952), pp. 2-3; The *Albatross*

(official publication of the White Motors Corp.) Vol. IX (1921), p. 4.

60. *Ibid.;* Interview with G.C. Frank, Assistant to the President, White Motors Corporation, Cleveland, Ohio, September 24, 1969.

61. *The Albatross* Vol. IX (1921), p. 24; Interview with G.C. Frank, September 24, 1969.

62. *White Steam Cars,* 1908 brochure (Cleveland: White Company, 1908), p. 4.

63. R.C. Carpenter, "Steam Plant of the White Motor Car," Paper presented at the New York meeting of the American Society of Mechanical Engineers, December, 1906 (New York: A.S.M.E., 1906), p. 5.

64. *White Steam Cars,* 1908 brochure, p. 14.

65. Carpenter, "Steam Plant of the White Car," p. 5.

66. *White Steam Cars,* 1910 brochure (Cleveland: White Company, 1910), pp. 5-7; J.E. Homans, *Self-Propelled Vehicles* (New York: T. Audel, 1908), p. 554.

67. Homans, *Self-Propelled Vehicles,* pp. 554-555; *White Steam Cars,* 1910, p. 8.

68. *White Steam Cars,* 1910, p. 5.

69. *Instructions for the White Steam Touring Car,* 1903 (Cleveland: White Sewing Machine Company, 1903), p. 2.

70. *White Steam Cars, 1906 Models* (Cleveland: White Company, 1906), p. 6.

71. *Ibid.,* p. 9.

72. *Instructions for the White Steam Cars, Models K and L,* 1908 (Cleveland: White Company, 1908), p. 10.

73. *Instructions for the White Steam Touring Car,* 1903, p. 12.

74. *White Steam Cars, 1908 Models,* pp. 9-10.

75. *Ibid.,* p. 10; *The White Steam Cars for 1905* (Cleveland: White Sewing Machine Company, 1905), p. 11.

76. Interview with G.C. Frank, September 24, 1969.

77. *White Steam Ambulances, Patrol Wagons and Buses,* 1909 (Cleveland: White Company, 1909), p. 2.

78. *Ibid.*

79. Superintendent Samuel Laughlin to the White Company, September 8, 1908, *Ibid.,* p. 7.

80. Commissioner Robert Hebberd to the White Company, September 4, 1908, *Ibid.,* p. 8.

81. *New York Herald,* November 24, 1907, p. 5.

82. *Ibid.; White Steam Ambulances,* p. 9.

83. Interview with G.C. Frank, September 24, 1969.

84. Mrs. G.A. Hawkins to the White Sewing Machine Company, *The Automobile* Vol. IX (October, 1906), p. 232.
85. *Ibid.*
86. *White Bulletin*, No. 12 (October, 1906), p. 23.
87. *Ibid.*, pp. 23-25.
88. The photograph collection is in the files of the Motor Vehicle Manufacturers Association, Detroit, Michigan.
89. *The Albatross* Vol. II (may, 1914), p. 5. In 1906 the automotive division of the White Sewing Machine Company was created as a separate branch. The White Sewing Machine Company is now known as the White Consolidated Industries with its main office in Cleveland, Ohio. There is no connection between the White Motor Corporation and the White Consolidated Industries.

IV/*One Hundred and Thirty-Four Others*

1. "Motor's Historical Table of the American Motor Car Industry," *Motor*, Vol. XI (March, 1909), pp. 36-42.
2. John B. Rae, *The American Automobile Manufacturers, The First Forty Years* (Philadelphia: Chilton, 1959), p. 3.
3. Georgano, *Encyclopaedia of Motorcars*, p. 315.
4. *Eagle*, (Poughkeepsie, N.Y.) January 3, 1941, p. 16.
5. *Ibid.*, p. 17; Interview with Susan T. Goodwin, granddaughter of William Lane, October 25, 1969.
6. Interview with Susan T. Goodwin, October 25, 1969.
7. *The Lane Automobiles*, 1903 brochure, (Poughkeepsie: Lane Motor Vehicle Company, 1903), p. 14.
8. *Ibid.*, p. 10.
9. *Ibid.*, p. 11.
10. *The Lane Steam Cars, Directions for Operating*, 1907, (Poughkeepsie: Lane Motor Vehicle Company, 1907), p. 14.
11. *Ibid.*, pp. 4-5.
12. Eleanor Lane Taylor to Susan T. Goodwin, November 16, 1969, Lane Family Collection.
13. *The Lane Automobiles*, 1903, p. 9.
14. *Clymer's Scrapbook, Steam Car Edition*, p. 67.
15. *Eagle*, (Poughkeepsie), January 3, 1941, p. 16; Interview with Susan T. Goodwin, October 25, 1969.
16. *Motor's 1907 Motor Car Directory* (New York: Motor Magazine, 1907), pp. 111-112.
17. Hugh Dolnar, "The 1905 Grout Steam Touring Car," *Cycle and*

Automobile Trade Journal Vol. IX (July 1, 1904), p. 56.

18. Carl S. Harwood (Balwinville, Mass.) to Author, October 7, 1970.

19. Dolnar, *Cycle and Automobile Trade Journal*, Vol. IX p. 58.

20. *Ibid.*; *The Grout Cars, 1905* (Orange, Massachusetts: Grout Brothers Automobile Company, 1905), p. 15.

21. Dolnar, *Cycle and Automobile Trade Journal*, Vol. IX, p. 59.

22. *Ibid.*

23. *The Grout Cars*, 1905, pp. 11-15.

24. *Clymer's Scrapbook, Steam Car Edition*, pp. 56, 61.

25. *New York Tribune*, January 28, 1900, p. 5.

26. Horseless Age, Vol. VIII, (September 11, 1901), p. 497.

27. *Ibid.*, p. 503.

28. *Clymer's Scrapbook, Steam Car Edition*, p. 48.

29. *Horseless Age*, Vol. XII, (June 24, 1903), p. 167.

30. *Ibid.*

31. *Stearns Steam Carriages, 1903 Models* (Syracuse: Stearns Steam Carriage Company, 1903), p. 4.

32. *Ibid.*; pp. 4-10; *Post-Standard* (Syracuse), August 26, 1900, p. 4.

33. *Stearns Steam Carriages, 1903 Models*, p. 2.

34. Harry Andrews Wright, *The Story of Western Massachusetts*, 4 vols. (New York: Lewis Historical Publishing Company, 1949), II, p. 841; The companies were Stevens-Duryea, Sultan, Atlas, Morse-Readio and Knox.

35. Georgano, *Encyclopaedia of Motorcars*, p. 427.

36. "The Victor," *Steam Automobile* Vol. VI (Summer, 1964), p. 10.

37. *Ibid.*, p. 11.

38. *Horseless Age* Vol. IX (April 23, 1902), p. 509.

39. *Ibid.*

40. Georgano, *Encyclopaedia of Motorcars*, p. 427.

41. *Gazette* (Taunton, Mass.), September 11, 1901, p. 3.

42. *Horseless Age*, Vol. IX (April 23, 1902), p. 509.

43. *Gazette* (Taunton), September 11, 1901, p. 3.

44. *Horseless Age*, Vol. IX (April 23, 1902), p. 509.

45. *Commercial and Financial Chronicle* Vol. LXX (May 5, 1900), p. 585; William Greenleaf, *Monopoly on Wheels* (Detroit: Wayne State University Press, 1961), p. 71.

46. John B. Rae, *The American Automobile Manufacturers*, p. 59.

47. Duncan, *World on Wheels*, I, p. 484.

48. Maurice D. Hendry, "The Steam Odyssey of Abner Doble," *Automobile Quarterly* Vol. VIII (Summer, 1969), p. 45.

49. Claude C. Hopkins, *My Life in Advertising* (Chicago: Advertising

Publications, 1966), p. 115.

50. James Doolittle, *The Romance of the Automobile Industry* (New York: Klebold Press, 1916), p. 31.

51. *Automobile Topics* Vol. I (October 20, 1900), p. 29.

52. *Horseless Age* Vol. VIII (November 20, 1901), p. 721.

53. *Floyd Clymer's Historical Motor Scrapbook, Steam Car Edition*, p. 46.

54. *Horseless Age* Vol. VIII (October 30, 1901), p. 634.

55. *Automobile Topics* Vol. III (November 16, 1901), p. 209.

56. *Horseless Age* Vol. VIII (October 30, 1901), p. 634; *Cycle and Automobile Trade Journal Supplement* Vol. VI, (November 1, 1901), p. 32C.

57. *Automobile Topics* Vol. III (November 16, 1901), p. 209.

58. *Cycle and Automobile Trade Journal*, Supplement Vol. III, (November 1, 1901), p. 32C.

59. *Ibid.*

60. *Motor World* Vol. V (January 22, 1903), p. 565.

61. *Geneva Daily Free Press* March 2, 1901, p. 3.

62. *Ibid.; Horseless Age* Vol. VIII (June 12, 1901), p. 221.

63. *Ibid.*, p. 217.

64. *Ibid.; Cycle and Automobile Trade Journal* Vol. VIII (March 1, 1903), p. 38.

65. *Ibid.*; Georgano, *Encyclopaedia of Motor Cars*, p. 244.

66. *Cycle and Automobile Trade Journal* Vol. VII (February 1, 1903), p. 38.

67. Byron Vazakas, "The Auto Industry in Reading," *Berks County Historical Review* Vol. IV (April, 1939), p. 68.

68. *Cycle and Automobile Trade Journal* Vol. VII (February 1, 1903), p. 97.

69. Vazakas, *Berks County Historical Review*, pp. 68-70.

70. *Ibid.*

71. *Ibid.*

72. *Cycle and Automobile Trade Journal* Vol. VIII (December 1, 1903), p. 26.

73. Vazakas, *Berks County Historical Review*, p. 69.

74. *Ibid.*

75. J.C. McClenathan, William Edie, Ellia Burgess, J.A. Coll, Eugene Norton, *Centennial History of the Borough of Connellsville* (Columbus: Champlin Press, 1906), p. 519.

76. *Ibid.*

77. *Motor Age* Vol. II (July 26, 1900), p. 696.

78. *Motor World* Vol. II (December, 1900), p. 3.

79. *Cycle and Automobile Trade Journal* Vol. VIII (October 8, 1903), p. 22.

80. *Ibid.* Vol. VIII (December 1, 1903), p. 61.

81. *Tribune-Republican*, Sesqui-centennial edition, (Meadville, Pennsylvania), 1938, p. 7.

82. *Ibid.*

83. Census of Manufactures, *Automobiles and Bicycles and Tricycles, 1905* (Washington, D.C.: Bureau of the Census, 1908), Bulletin 66.

84. Department of Commerce and Labor, *Motor Vehicles, Special Consular Reports* (Washington, D.C.: Government Printing Office, 1908), Vol. XL, part 2

85. *Ford Motor Cars, 1908 Models N, S and K* reprint (Los Angeles: Clymer Publications, 1951), p. 6.

86. Niemeyer, *Automotive Career of Ransom Olds*, p. 52.

87. *Horseless Age* Vol. V (December 6, 1899), p. 12.

88. Eugene F. Hord, "History and Organization of Automobile Insurance," Paper delivered before the Insurance Society of New York, November 11 and 18, 1919, p. 9.

89. Ralph C. Epstein, "The Rise and Fall of Firms in the Automobile Industry," *Harvard Business Review* Vol. V (January, 1927), p. 161.

90. Doolittle, *Romance of the Automobile Industry*, p. 286.

V/The Fastest Cars in the World

1. "The President in his White," advertising circular, (Cleveland: White Company, 1909).

2. *White Bulletin*, No. 16 (October, 1909), p. 3.

3. *Ibid.*, p. 19.

4. *Ibid.*, p. 21.

5. Association of Licensed Automobile Manufacturers, *Handbook of Gasoline Automobiles* (New York: A.L.A.M., 1909), pp. 1-139. The A.L.A.M. was organized to protect makers of gas cars. In 1903, the auto makers of the day agreed to recognize the validity of the Selden patent thereby protecting themselves, their dealers and their users by securing license under the patent.

6. Doolittle, *Romance of the Automobile*, p. 84.

7. *White Steam Cars*, 1908, p. 2.

8. *Horseless Age*, Vol. XVI (November 1, 1905), p. 499.

9. *Ibid.*, p. 500.

10. *Ibid.*, p. 501.

11. *Ibid.*, p. 502.

12. *Ibid.*, p. 505.

13. Lionel S. Marks, *Gas and Oil Engines* (Chicago: American School of Correspondence, 1906), p. 51.

14. J.E. Homans, *Self-Propelled Vehicles*, p. 160.

15. *Motor Age* Vol. XLI (May 11, 1922), p. 43.

16. *"Pointed Questions and Direct Answers Covering the Stanley Car* (Newton: Stanley Motor Carriage Company, 1922), pp. 17-18.

17. George Woodbury, *The Story of a Stanley Steamer*, p. 212.

18. *Steam Motor Journal*, Vol. V (July, 1907), p. 10.

19. *Horseless Age* Vol. XIII (January 3, 1904), p. 48.

20. Oscar C. Schmidt (ed.), *Practical Treatise on Automobiles* 2 vols. (Philadelphia: American Textbook Company, 1911), Vol. I, p. 238.

21. *Ibid.*, I, p. 242.

22. *Ibid.*, I, p. 244.

23. *Motor Field*, Vol. XX (February, 1907), p. 87.

24. David Hebb, "No Punctures, No Blowouts," *Automobile Quarterly* Vol. II (Summer, 1963), pp. 225-227.

25. Homans, *Self-Propelled Vehicles*, p. 562.

26. Schmidt, *Treatise on Automobiles*, I, p. 186.

27. Doolittle, *Romance of the Automobile Industry*, p. 39.

28. *Ibid.*

29. *Cleveland Plain Dealer*, June 29, 1897, p. 1; Doolittle, *Romance of the Automobile Industry*, p. 322.

30. Doolittle, *Romance of the Automobile Industry*, p. 322; *Scientific American* Vol. LXXX (July 24, 1897), p. 300.

31. *Horseless Age*, Vol. VIII (July 31, 1901), p. 261.

32. *Motor World*, Vol. II (May 8, 1901), p. 9.

33. *Horseless Age*, Vol. VIII (July 31, 1901), p. 261.

34. *Automobile* Vol. III (October, 1901), p. 893.

35. *Ibid.*, p. 894.

36. *Horseless Age*, Vol. VIII (May 29, 1901), p. 206.

37. *Ibid.*, Vol. IX (March 12, 1902), p. 346.

38. Secretary of State, *Highway Law of the State of New York* (Albany: T.B. Lyon, Printer, 1913), p. 70.

39. *Horseless Age* Vol. IX (June 18, 1902), p. 726.

40. *Ibid.*

41. *Ibid.*, Vol. XII (July 15, 1903), p. 62.

42. *Ibid.*; at the time gasoline cost between ten and fifteen cents per gallon compared to seven cents a gallon for kerosene.

43. "White Racers," *Steam Automobile* Vol. IX (May, 1967), p. 314.

44. *Ibid.*, p. 315; *White Bulletin* No. 8 (January, 1905), p. 7.

45. *White Bulletin* No. 1 (October, 1903), p. 7.

46. *Ibid.*

47. *Ibid.*, p. 8.

48. *Ibid.*, No. 8 (January, 1905), p. 14.

49. Anthony Bird and Francis Hutton Stott (eds.), *The Veteran Motor Car Pocketbook* (London: B.T. Batsford, 1963), p. 242.

50. Prescott Warren to the Editor of *Scientific American* December 17, 1916, *A Discussion About the Steam Car* pamphlet reprinted (Chicago: Steam Automobile Club of America, 1963), p. 18.

51. *Ibid.*

52. *Steam Automobile*, Vol. IX, p. 314.

53. *Ibid.*

54. *Automobile* Vol. XIV (October 8, 1904), p. 32.

55. *Cleveland Plain Dealer*, October 16, 1904, p. 4; *Steam Automobile*, Vol. IX, p. 317.

56. *Brooklyn Daily Eagle*, November 25, 1905, p. 6.

57. *White Bulletin* No. 16 (October, 1909), p. 16.

58. *Stanley, 1908 Models*, p. 22.

59. *Ibid.*

60. *Automobile* Vol. XIII (June 16, 1903), p. 588.

61. *Ibid.*

62. *Ibid.*

63. *Ibid.*, p. 589.

64. *Ibid.*

65. *Ibid.*

66. *Floyd Clymer's Historical Motor Scrapbook, Steam Car Edition*, p. 70; *Scientific American* Vol. XCIIII (February 3, 1906), p. 36; The Stanley racer was rated at 50 horsepower by A.L.A.M. standards, but could develop 250 horsepower at maximum revolutions per minute.

67. *Scientific American* Vol. XCIII (February 3, 1906), p. 36; Raymond W. Stanley, *Automobile Quarterly*, Vol. II p. 123; American Automobile Association, *Official Record Book* (Los Angeles, Clymer Publications, 1950), p. 50.

68. *Official Record Book*, p. 50.

69. Stanley, *Automobile Quarterly*, Vol. II, p. 124.

70. *Ibid.*

71. Frederick Wagner, *Saga of the Roaring Road* (Los Angeles: Clymer Publications, 1949), p. 86.

72. Stanley, *Automobile Quarterly*, Vol. II, p. 126.

73. *Ibid.*, p. 128.

74. *Lane Automobiles*, 1903, pp. 2-3.
75. *Automobiles of America*, p. 23.
76. Wagner, *Saga of the Roaring Road*, p. 83.
77. *Ibid.*
78. John Bently, *Great American Automobiles* (Englewood Cliffs, New Jersey: Prentice-Hall, 1957), p. 35.
79. Official Record Book, p. 50.
80. J.D. Nies to the *Editor of the Scientific American* October 30, 1916, *A Discussion About the Steam Car*, p. 24.
81. A.B. Browne and E.H. Lockwood, "The Practical Testing of Motor Vehicles," *Transactions of the Society of Automotive Engineers*, Vol. X, Part I, p. 87.

VI/The Last of the Many

1. *Automobile Trade Journal* Vol. XXIX (May 20, 1924), p. 687.
2. Maurice D. Hendry, *Automobile Quarterly*, Vol. VIII, p. 45.
3. *Ibid.*, p. 43.
4. J.N. Walton, *Doble Steam Cars, Buses, Trucks, Lories* (York, England: Horne and Son, 1959), p. 5.
5. *Ibid.*, p. 4: In the simple expansion type engine steam moves in but one direction in the cylinder, entering through the inlet passage, expanding against the piston head and then passing out of the exhaust ports.
6. *Ibid.*
7. *Horseless Age* Vol. XXXIV (September 15, 1916), p. 205.
8. *Ibid.*
9. *Ibid.*
10. *Automobile* Vol. XXXII (September 7, 1916), p. 410; Maurice D. Hendry, *Automobile Quarterly*, Vol. VIII, p. 49.
11. *Announcement of the Doble-Detroit Steam Motors Company* 1917 (Detroit: General Engineering Company, 1917), p. 4.
12. *Ibid.*, p.
13. *Detroit News*, May 10, 1917, p. 3.
14. *Ibid.*
15. *Ibid.*
16. *Ibid.*
17. *Announcement of Doble-Detroit*, p. 4.
18. Walton, *Doble Steam Cars*, pp. 12-14; *Bulletin*, (San Francisco), July 2, 1921, p. 7.

19. Walton, *Doble Steam Cars*, p. 17.

20. R.A. Wilson to Mr. Hartman, October 19, 1922, *Ibid.*, p. 19.

21. *The Doble Steam Car*, 1923 Models, reprint (Los Angeles: Clymer Publications, 1951), p. 10.

22. Walton, *Doble Steam Cars*, p. 30.

23. *The Doble Steam Car, 1923 Models*, p. 10.

24. *Ibid.*, p. 14.

25. Walton, *Doble Steam Cars*, pp. 22-23; Barney Becker, "Doble Notes," *Steam Automobile*, Vol. XII, p. 17.

26. Walton, *Doble Steam Cars*, p. 23.

27. *Announcement of the Doble Steam Motors Corporation* (Los Angeles: E.G. Cox Inc., 1922), p. 13.

28. Hendry, *Automobile Quarterly*, Vol. VIII, p. 17.

29. Barney Becker, *Steam Automobile*, Vol. XII, p. 17.

30. *The Doble Steam Car* 1923 Models pp. 3-6; *Motor* (England) Vol. LXX (November 20, 1923), p. 817.

31. National Automotive Chamber of Commerce, *Handbook of Automobiles 1924* (New York: N.A.C.C., 1924), pp. 20, 70, 88.

32. Hendry, *Automobile Quarterly* Vol. VIII, p. 56.

33. Walton, *Doble Steam Cars*, pp. 53, 56-57; *Motor Age* Vol. XLI (June 22, 1922), p. 35.

34. *Announcement of the Doble Steam Motors*, p. 11) *Motor Age* Vol. XLI (June 22, 1922), p. 35.

35. Hendry, *Automobile Quarterly* Vol. VIII, p. 58.

36. *Ibid.*, p. 59; Derr, *The Modern Steam Car*, p. 137; George and William Bessler acquired the Doble patents and continued to develop the inventor's projects. Abner and Warren Doble worked on steam projects in England, Germany and New Zealand. In the 1950's Abner became involved with the Paxton Phoenix and Keen steam cars. He died in 1961.

37. "Again the Steam Automobile," *Scientific American* Vol. CXXII (February 28, 1920), p. 220.

38. Chamber of Commerce, *Bulletin of the Camden Chamber of Commerce* (Camden: Chamber of Commerce, 1924), p. 56.

39. *Brooks Steamer*, 1923 reprint, (Los Angeles: Clymer Publication, 1950), 2.

40. *The One Thousand Dollar Steam Automobile* 1922 brochure (Indianapolis, Indiana: George A. Coats Machine Company, 1922), p. 1.

41. *Coats Steam Power*, 1922 brochure (Chicago: Coats Steam Car Company, 1922), p. 1.

42. *Motor Age* Vol. XLIII (May 24, 1923), p. 37.

43. *Automobile Trade Journal* XXVII (June 1, 1923), p. 100.
44. *Floyd Clymer's Historical Motor Scrapbook, Steam Car Edition*, p. 180.
45. "A Steamer Without a Differential," *Motor* Vol. XXXVII (December, 1921), p. 36.
46. *Scientific American* Vol. CXXII, p. 221.
47. *Baker Steam Boiler* 1922 brochure, reprint (Los Angeles: Floyd Clymer, 1954), p. 1.
48. *Delling Steam Car*, 1921 reprint (Los Angeles: Floyd Clymer, 1954), p. 4.
49. "Will the Steam Automobile Return?" *Scientific American* Vol. CXXXVIII (January, 1928), pp. 44-45.
50. *Ibid.*
51. *Ibid.*
52. *Ibid.*
53. *Automotive Industries* Vol. XLVIII (June 7, 1923), p. 1242.
54. Federal Trade Commission, *Report on the Motor Vehicle Industry* (Washington, D.C.: Government Printing Office, 1939), pp. 643-645.
55. *Motor* (England) Vol. CX (December, 1951), p. 29.
56. A.L. Dyke, *Dyke's Automobile and Gasoline Engine Encyclopaedia* 12th edition (Chicago: Goodheart, Wilcox, 1943), pp. 224-226.
57. *Ibid.*
58. Walton, *Doble Steam Cars*, p. 39.
59. Ralph Andreano, Harold Williamson, Arnold Daum, Gilbert Close *The Age of Illumination* Vol. I of *The American Petroleum Industry*, 2 vols. (Evanston, Illinois: Northwestern University Press, 1963), p. 195.

VII/The Battle Is Over

1. J.D. Nies to Editor, October 30, 1916, *Scientific American* Vol. II (November 25, 1916), p. 301.
2. A.B. Browne and R.H. Lockwood, "The Practical Testing of Motor Vehicles," *Transactions of the Society of Automotive Engineers*, Vol. X Part 1. p. 67.
3. *1909 Instruction Book, Reo Touring Car and Roadster* reprint, (Los Angeles: Clymer Publications, 1951), p. 15.
4. *1909 Instruction Book, Maxwell Models E, Q, G.* reprint, (Los Angeles: Clymer Publications, 1951), pp. 2-3.
5. *1909 Instruction Book Packard 30 B and 18*, reprint, (Los Angeles: Clymer Publications, 1951), p. 45.
6. *Automobiles of America*, p. 54.

7. *Stanley Steam Cars, Announcement for the Season of 1916* (Newton: Stanley Motor Carriage Company, 1916), p. 6; *Questions and Answers on Stanley Steamers* (Newton: Stanley Motor Carriage Company, 1920), pp. 16-17.

8. *Questions and Answers on Stanley Steamers*, pp. 16-17.

9. A.L. Clough, "Steam and Gasoline Vehicles Compared," *Horseless Age* Vol. XII (July 8, 1903), p. 30.

10. Lionel S. Marks, *Gas and Oil Engines* (Chicago: American School of Correspondence, 1906), pp. 2-3.

11. *Ibid.*, p. 4.

12. Walton, *Doble Steam Cars*, p. 30.

13. Joseph Zmuda, "Blowing the Steam Dream," *Motor Trend* Vol. XXI (November, 1969), p. 45.

14. Lawrence Seltzer, *A Financial History of the American Automobile Industry* (Boston: Houghton Mifflin, 1928), p. 26.

15. Hopkins, *My Life in Advertising*, p. 119.

16. Albert L. Clough, "Steam and Gasoline Vehicles Compared," *Horseless Age* Vol. XII (July 22, 1903), p. 82.

17. *Ibid.*, Vol. XVIII (August 15, 1906), p. 204.

18. *Ibid.*, p. 204.

VII/Steam Now

1. *New York Times*, March 30, 1970, p. 33.

2. *Steam Automobile* Vol. II (1969), p. 5.

3. *New York Times*, March 12, 1971, p. 27.

4. Donald E. Carr, *The Breath of Life* (New York: Berkeley Medallion Books, 1970), p. 98.

5. *Facts on File* Vol. XXI (May 13-19, 1971), p. 373.

6. *Ibid.* Vol. XXXI (May 13-19, 1971).

7. *Cleaner Air for the Nation*, p. 11; *Automotive News*, April 16, 1973, p. 46.

8. Chapter 418, *Laws of New Jersey, 1971*, Assembly Number 2181, p. 1.

9. "Quiet Please," *Newsweek Magazine* Vol. 79 (February 7, 1972), p. 45.

10. *Ibid.*

11. *Ibid.*

12. "Supreme Muffler," Advertisement *Motor Trend* Vol. XXII, (August, 1970), p. 100.

13. "Arvin Muffler," advertisement *Ibid.*, p. 84.

14. Charles G. Burck, "Detroit Turns Against the Gas Guzzlers," *Fortune* Vol. LXXXIX (January, 1974), p. 98.

15. *"William P. Lear, the Man and the Commitment,* (Reno: Lear Motors Corp., 1971), p. 2.

16. *Alternatives to the Gasoline-Powered Internal Combustion Engine*, p. 83; Ronald Schiller, "Bill Lear, Inventor of the Impossible," *Reader's Digest* Vol. XCIX (August, 1971), pp. 148-149.

17. *Lear, The Man and the Commitment*, p. 3.

18. *Automotive News*, July 10, 1972, p. 4.

19. *Lear, the Man and the Commitment*, p. 5.

20. *Steam Bus Symposium Proceedings*, p. 56.

21. *Steam Bus Newsletter* Vol. 4, (January 10, 1972), p. 6.

22. *Automotive News*, July 10, 1972, p. 4.

23. "Floridian says Engine May Stop Air Pollution," *New York Times*, September 6, 1970, p. 14.

24. *Ibid.*; Minto is also credited with developing an ultraviolet flashlight for spotting numerals at night, a light-reflecting material used in airport runways and a gadget that detects metal in deep water.

25. *Alternatives to the Gasoline-Powered Internal Combustion Engine*, p. 71.

26. *Ibid.*, p. 71.

27. *Ibid.*

28. *Ibid.*

29. *New York Times*, September 6, 1970, p. 14.

30. Elliot Miles, "Steam Today, The New Generation of Puffers," *Automobile Quarterly* Vol. VIII, (Summer, 1969), p. 62.

31. *Ibid.*

32. *Ibid.*, p. 63.

33. *Philadelphia Enquirer*, September 21, 1971, p. 8.

34. *Ibid.*

35. Elliot Miles, *Automobile Quarterly*, Vol. VIII, p. 62.

36. *Steam Automobile* Vol. 12, (1970), p. 1.

37. *Alternatives to the Gasoline-Powered Internal Combustion Engine*, p. 28.

38. *Ibid.*, p. 28.

39. *Ibid.*, pp. 38-39.

40. *Ibid.*, p. 41.

41. Pedr Davis, "Steamer Seeks Speed Mark," *Automotive News*, January 25, 1971, p. 2.

42. *Ibid.*

43. "Green Light on Smogless Car," *Saturday Review* Vol. III (Dec. 6, 1969), p. 84.

44. *The Steam Automobile*, Vol. 12 (1970), p. I.

45. "Statement of Geni Power Inc.," printed by *Steam Automobile*, Vol. October, 1971, p. 7.

46. *Ibid.*

47. *Steam Bus Newsletter*, Vol. IV, (January 10, 1972), p. 1.

48. *Ibid., p. 5.*

49. *Ibid.*

50. *Steam Bus Symposium Proceedings*, p. 30.

51. *Ibid.*, p. 32.

52. *Alternatives to the Gasoline-Powered Internal Combustion Engine*, p. 72.

53. *Ibid.*

54. *Ibid.*, p. 71.

55. *Report of the President's Task Force on Air Pollution*, p. 16.

56. *Automotive News*, December 6, 1971, p. 1.

57. *New York Times*, April 9, 1972, p. 68.

58. A.B. Shuman, "The Anatomy of a Rotary," *Motor Trend* Vol. XXIV, (November 1972), p. 71.

59. "The Wankel-engined Mazda RX2," *Consumer Reports* Vol. 37, April, 1972), p. 213.

60. *Ibid.*, p. 212.

61. *Ibid.*, p. 213.

62. *Ibid.*

63. "Lead Residue seen Threat to Catalytic Converters," *Automotive News*, January 3, 1972, p. 3.

64. *New York Times*, October 11, 1970, p. 86.

65. Texas Eastern Transmission Corp., *Pyrofax Gas, Facts and Figures on the Clean Air Question* (1972). p. 2.

66. *Ibid.*, p. 4.

67. *Ibid.*, p. 3.

68. *New York Times*, July 11, 1970, p. 11.

69. *Ibid.*

70. *Ibid.*

71. *Ibid.*

72. *Wall Street Journal*, August 9, 1972, p. 6.

73. *New York Times*, August 9, 1972, p. 47; R. Tom Sawyer, *The Modern Gas Turbine* (New York-Prentice-Hall, 1945), pp. 19-20.

74. *New York Times* August 9, 1972, p. 6.

75. *Wall Street Journal*, August 9, 1972, p. 6.

76. John W. Riley, "Ford Looks in on Steam Project," *Automotive*

News, November 20, 1972, p. 49.

77. *Ibid.*

78. *Ibid.*

79. "Anderson Power Products" advertisement in *Electric Vehicle News* Vol. 1 (August 19, 1972), p. 9.

80. *Ibid.* p. 23.

81. *Ibid.*

82. *Alternatives to the Gasoline-Powered Internal Combustion Engine,* p. 2.

83. *Ibid.*

84. *Ibid.,* p. 7.

85. *Automotive News,* July 29, 1972, p. 3; June 4, 1973, p. 1.

86. *Ibid.,* November 6, 1972, pp. 2, 65.

87. Jan P. Norbye and Jim Dunne, "Honda's New CVCC Car Engine Meets '75 Emission Standards Now," *Popular Science,* Vol. CCII, April, 1973, p. 80.

88. *Automotive News,* November 29, 1972, p. 18.

89. *New York Times,* November 5, 1972, p. 17.

90. *Ibid.*

91. *Ibid.,* January 14, 1973, p. 41.

Acknowledgments

Figure 5: courtesy Mrs. H. Sage Goodwin, Lane Family Collection; figures 9 and 11: courtesy White Motors Corporation; figure 13: *Motor Age,* July 1900; figure 19: *Steam Bus Symposium Proceedings,* November 17, 1971.